Bless Your Little Cotton Socks

Bless Your Little Cotton Socks

Beyond the Quirky Sayings of My Eccentric Scottish Mum

DIANE RADFORD

authorHOUSE®

AuthorHouse™
1663 Liberty Drive
Bloomington, IN 47403
www.authorhouse.com
Phone: 1 (800) 839-8640

Published by AuthorHouse 01/11/2017

ISBN: 978-1-5246-5257-9 (sc)
ISBN: 978-1-5246-5258-6 (hc)
ISBN: 978-1-5246-5256-2 (e)

Library of Congress Control Number: 2016919880

Print information available on the last page.

This book is printed on acid-free paper.

Dedication

For Pam
In memory of Margery and Sidney

Table of Contents

Introduction ix

Part One: Hunter Crescent 1

But Mistinguett is Dead 3
That Dog Cost Twenty Guineas 8
The Kittens Are in the Oven Under a Low Gas 11
We've Arrived, and to Prove it, We're Here 13
Have a Chitter-Bite 15
The Animal Must Roam Free 18
A Golden Treasury of Verse 21
Reading Love Letters 25
I'm Taking Some Brandy to the Guinea Pigs 27
There's a Grave Danger You'll Live 29

Part Two: Bentinck Drive 33

Worse Things Happen At Sea 34
Margery on Wheels 38
The General's Rooms 42
Wee Sleekit Cow'rin Tim'rous Beastie 46
Bond...James Bond 51
Fireballs in my Eucharist 54
What Did Your Last Servant Die Of? 58
They're Knot 60
Give the Child Some Laudanum 65
An Irish Mess 67

The Open Championship 69

The Mother Formerly Known as Margery............................... 72

A Pause for Silent Prayer... 75

Dodds Coach Trip 78

The Things You See When You Don't Have Your Gun 81

Gin a Body, Meet a Body. 84

Part Three: Wilson Avenue 89

The Skelington... 90

Bonnets Over the Windmill.. 93

A Chance to Remember 95

Part Four: Marine View Court.. 129

Taxi-Parade 130

There Was a War On 132

Part Five: Sandilands... 137

The Sleeping Warrior 139

Patter-Merchant 140

A Unit of Measurement.. 143

Funny Ha-Ha or Funny Peculiar 145

Part Six: Dallas Place, Princes Square, and Westbank 149

Elegant Sufficiency... 151

Old Buggerlugs 153

Bless Your Little Cotton Socks 159

Epilogue: The Bench... 165

Acknowledgements.. 167

About the Author 169

Endorsements.. 171

Introduction

This is essentially a happy book. All right, there are some sad episodes, but as my mother Margery would explain, if she were here, these are the vagaries and vicissitudes of life (she had a polysyllabic way about her). To expect everything to be rosy all the time is just not realistic. My parents, Margery and Sidney, were honest, hard-working folk—pragmatists, as would be expected from their north-of-England upbringing. When I read memoirs of other people's childhoods, they are often full of tragedy: alcoholism, abuse, and abandonment. Contrary to these upbringings, my father wasn't an alcoholic, though Mum did enjoy the odd tipple. I did not develop irritating tics, turn to drugs, or sell myself for extra lucre. I grieved when they died, but among my last words to each of them were, "I love you," and for that, I am grateful.

In the years since my mother's death, I have found myself beginning sentences with "as my mother would have said," or "as Margery would say," followed by one of her pithy comments, always apropos. The concept for this book began with me shuffling hangers in the hall closet on my fiftieth birthday, and discovering the earth-toned jacket she wore as protection against the gusting wind of Troon, on the west coast of Scotland, where my parents moved in the mid 1950s. Once I left home, no matter where I was living, it was her habit—and I have to say I loved it—to call me every year on my birthday and recite the events of my almost-didn't-make-it birth in the nearby town of Irvine. Her story ended with the punch line, "But Mistinguett is dead," Mistiguett being a famous French dancer in the 1930s, the original showgirl, famed for her legs. As I held my mother's jacket, a couple of years after her death, her words resonated in my mind. Replacing the garment in the closet, I hurried to my desk and wrote down her words. In the months and years that followed, I compiled a list of this and other "Margeryisms." Some of her quirky sayings were of her own creation—pure Margery; others were those she adopted and adapted. One of my favorite phrases of hers was her goodbye blessing, "Bless your little cotton socks."

I created lists all over the place—on napkins, on index cards, in my calendar, and on my desk. Margery helped me write this book. I can still hear the way she intoned a sentence; I picture her mannerisms and facial expressions. Sometimes she gestured in a grandiose fashion. Not uncommonly, she would trill "tra-la," her hand spiraling through the air to demonstrate her point.

I never realized quite how much my mother differed from other mothers until I began to quote her when I moved to America, and people responded with either a quizzical stare or a peal of laughter. I had presumed everyone had a mother who would demonstrate the Charleston in the middle of doing dishes—suds flying across the kitchen—or recite Masefield's "Ships" on a walk along the shore.

As my mother and I ambled along the dunes one July day in 1972 linked arm in arm, a lark winged skyward above the golf course, singing gloriously. Another soon followed. "Aha," Margery said as she craned her neck to watch, "an exultation of larks." Even a walk along the dunes provided an educational opportunity for this primary school teacher. She continued her exposition of avian collective nouns: "a gaggle of geese, a murder of crows, a covey of quail, a parliament of owls, a congregation of plovers." She would have gone on, but I started laughing and then we were both giggling as we strolled along, our shoulders shaking.

Not only is an exultation the plural form of lark, but it was also the way Margery lived life. She loved life with infectious exuberance. I looked forward to those walks, not just for the exercise, but also for the closeness to her, the way she pointed things out along the way—whether it be a razor shell on the moist sand or a pair of orange-beaked oystercatchers along the shoreline, their black and white feathers formal as a tuxedo.

I grew up in one of the most beautiful places on earth, which forms the backdrop for a great many of the memories that make up these essays. Mother loved its beauty, too, not just Troon, but the whole of Scotland. Although she was born in England, she lived more of her life in Scotland, and would call herself a Scot if anyone asked. Even so, Margery had a wanderlust that left her unsettled with whatever house was her current abode; hence, she and Sid moved frequently—eight homes in all in Troon. Of course, many of these homes were my home, too, and I have divided this book into parts according to where we or they were living at the time.

Troon, and our travels within it and beyond, shaped me, as much as my parents did. My childhood was filled with walks on the beach, feeding the birds; golf on the narrowest fairways between banks of yellow broom; the dog, cat, hamster, rabbit, sticklebacks, and frogspawn; and the Daleks.

These reminiscences of my childhood revealed to me I was altogether blessed—not just my cotton socks.

Part One

Hunter Crescent

Margery and Sidney's first home in Troon (and mine, too) was a brick ranch house that stood beside the lane connecting Hunter Crescent to Dundonald Road. A tall brick wall divided our back garden from the lane, but a large wooden gate allowed entry. Pass through, and you would see to the right a vegetable patch containing rhubarb and gooseberries. The leaves of the rhubarb unfurled to provide cover, an exciting, if grubby, hiding place when I was still small enough. Sometimes I'd eat the gooseberries right off the bushes, not minding their tartness and prickly skin.

Rimming the expanse of lawn, on the left, was the luxuriant copper beech hedge that separated our property from the neighbors' to the rear. In the center of the grass was a low sand pit, the walls about eight inches high. My next-door neighbor William and I would make sand castles and play fort, sometimes bringing out soldiers from our respective toy boxes. The other edge of the garden abutted the burn, from which water voles would wander into the garden. It was the best burn for sticklebacks and frogspawn. The windowsill in the kitchen was home to a legion of sentry-like jam jars, containing frogs in various phases of metamorphosis.

On the crescent side of the house, a low wall divided the rose beds from the sidewalk. It was on that low wall that I would stand, looking towards Wilson Avenue, when Auntie Joan came to visit, attentive for the throaty roar of her white MG BGT. She called her sports car "Baby Love." When it was replaced, she named her new car "Baby Love Two." Mum filled the front garden with rose bushes—her favorites were pink, red, and white—and then complained about having to prune them. She was forever

1

toiling in the garden; her feet shod in wellies, spade in hand, turning over the musty, thick soil for planting. The driveway to the detached single car garage was to the left of the house. When I was about nine, my parents decided they needed more space and converted the attic into two bedrooms and a bathroom. The staircase was an open design in teak, so open I was terrified of falling through.

Our neighbors along the crescent included the Whytocks, the Holmeses, the Walkers, the Cooks, the Thompsons, and the Frews, close friends of Dad and Mum since their days in Milngavie, near Glasgow, where Mum and Mary Frew were teachers together. The Frews lived next to the horses' field, where the Martins from Dunchattan House, one of the grand old estates still in existence, often kept their horses. Alastair Frew kept a large aviary in the rear of his property, which I thought was the epitome of exotic.

Walking in the other direction along the crescent, away from the Frew's home, one would encounter the long driveway lined by lush greenery and rhododendrons that leads to the site of Fullarton House. The mansion house was demolished in the early 1960s, however the stables were preserved.

The house on Hunter Crescent was my first home, and my memories of it are especially rich.

But Mistinguett is Dead

My mother had great legs. She was especially proud of her trim ankles—dancer's ankles. Her ankles led to well-shaped calves and perfectly-formed knees.

Six years old, tucked into a corner of the room wallpapered with painted anaglypta to the front of the house on Hunter Crescent, I observed my mother's ritual of putting on her stockings as she dressed for a dinner dance.

Placing one foot on the seat of the low nursing chair, she stretched the stocking, bunched up in two hands, over her toes, its toe over her toes, and brought the delicate, shimmery 15-dernier sheen upwards, smoothing it as she went, arching her foot—an action that accentuated her calves. When it reached her thigh, she snapped the top of it to her garter belt. This was the early 1960s, before pantyhose.

Glancing over at me, she placed a hand on the gap of porcelain thigh between the top of her stocking and the leg of her underpants. "Do you know what your Auntie Joan calls this?" Not a real Auntie, Joan was one of my godmothers, and the most glamorous creature in my world. The christening photos show her holding me on her lap, urging me to look at the camera. Her hair is elegantly coiffed, the charm bracelet around her wrist holding my attention. I'm not looking at the camera; I'm fixated on her, mesmerized. I shook my head no to my mother's question.

"She calls it the giggle gap." She carried on, after a look at my puzzled face. "Because if a man gets there, he's laughing." She tossed her head back, chuckling at the thought, and wiggled into her skirt, completing the tiered array of waistlines, underpants, suspender belt, and skirt.

Such was my introduction to the giggle gap. A lot to take in at six.

My parents Margery and Sidney were a social couple. I recall that a sitter came over to mind me weekly while the parental unit gadded about town. Family albums provide the proof: snaps and formal photos taken at the dinner dances at the Marine Hotel in Troon, the Rotary Club events at the Suncourt Hotel, and the Teachers' dances. They are decked out, Mum with her hair recently set at Morgenthaler's on Portland Street, long white gloves, dangly earrings, a fur stole around her shoulders, sometimes a tiara. In the photos, she has her feet placed just so, with one satiny shoe partly behind the other, showing off her aforementioned trim ankles. Dad looks handsome in his tux and cummerbund, his shoulders broad and pulled back. Their hair glistens courtesy of Schwarzkopf and Brylcream. In some of the photos Mum balances a cigarette between her fingers, smoke drifting upwards.

When they returned home from these events, still in dancing mood, albeit a bit wobbly, they pushed the furniture to the periphery of the living room and glided over the parquet floor, Mum with a rose between her teeth. The budgie, or parakeet, cocked its head sideways from its elevated perch and bobbed as if timed with the music from the gramophone. In my pyjamas and holding Edward Bear, I peered from a darkened corner, entranced by the scene.

My mother's love of dancing flooded my memory on my fiftieth birthday as I sorted through the hall closet picking out winter coats for dry cleaning. I'd been rummaging through pockets, finding show tickets from the previous winter (what a good show that was), money, old tissues, cough drop wrappers, when there it was: my mother's jacket, the one she wore for golf, waiting for me on the next hanger. Salmon, some might call it peach, it is a lovely color, earthy, a bit like the red rocks of Sedona.

I can see her wearing it in my mind's eye, teeing up, taking her stance against the blustery wind. The manufacturer is Grenfell™, 67% terylene and—once upon a time—waterproof. Now if it rains when I wear it, my shoulders get wet, but I don't mind. She had another one in turquoise for gardening. I can see her in the garden, leaning proudly against a shovel, my dad beside her, sleeves rolled up, the dog Pepe at their feet looking up. It's the "We have conquered the garden" look. They smile at the camera, a team. The gardening jacket is long gone, its life expectancy much shorter than that worn for golf. I so loved the colors of her jackets that I had a custom road bike painted peach and turquoise to reproduce those hues.

As I took the earth-toned jacket off its hanger and held it close, I remembered the phone call I received every year on my birthday.

"Do you know what I was doing (however many it was) years ago today?"

"What were you doing," I replied, knowing the answer full well.

"I was having my C-section."

Then would come the story. I never tired of it—the recital about the pre-eclampsia, the fact that at forty-three she was an elderly primagravida, the month of bed rest, the low salt diet, the choice of dates for the surgery (the 14th or the 15th, sometimes she had to ask me in order to remember the correct date), the operation itself, my arrival at 3lbs 12 oz (my lightest weight ever), the month in the makeshift incubator, not being able to go home till I weighed 5lbs, special food sent over the Atlantic from Canada, her Ob palpating her ankles daily and saying, "Mrs. Radford, your ankles are not swollen; you have legs like Mistinguett," and her high-pitched reply, "But Mistinguett is dead!"

Mistinguett (pronounced Miss-tahn-get) was a great French singer and dancer, renowned for her enviably slim ankles. She was the original showgirl, resplendent in feathered headdresses, and her legs were legendary. In 1919, she insured them for 500,000 francs. She entertained at the famous nightclubs, Casino de Paris and the Moulin Rouge, and at one time, she was the highest paid entertainer in the world. The sculptor Rodin (of The Kiss and The Thinker) purportedly once said to Mistinguett, "If I had to personify the Muse of the Music Hall, I would give her your legs, Mistinguett."

So to say my mother had legs like Mistinguett was to say that she had the best legs in the world. Dr. DeSoldenhoff had extended a great compliment. The French entertainer had just passed away, at the grand age of eighty, the year prior to my being ripped untimely from the womb.

Not only was Mother miffed at the idea that she had the legs of a deceased person, but she was none too thrilled about being described as an "elderly primagravida." I can imagine the penetrating gaze she fixed on the Belgian obstetrician when he first used that term with her to describe a woman who was older than thirty-five at the time of her first pregnancy.

In the retelling each year, my mother's voice would climb a few decibels, "Elderly? But I am in my prime," she would declare, Miss Jean Brodie-esque. I'm sure his brow must have arched over his monacled right eye at this retort.

Dr. DeSoldenhoff's avuncular calm covered his underlying concern. Pre-eclampsia is a potentially life-threatening condition during gestation. Characterized by a rapid rise in blood pressure, it can progress to seizures, and ultimately death for both mother and baby. My mother was hospitalized immediately following the diagnosis and weighed daily. Her placenta began to fail. "You were losing weight in utero," she said of me. The good doctor who examined her daily checked for pitting edema of the ankles, seeing if his fingers dented her tissue. Cesarean section or induction of labor can be required to prevent a crisis of high blood pressure.

For 1957 I was a great save. The placenta had not failed completely; there had been no seizures; both mother and child survived. Dr. DeSoldenhoff was proud. The Chief of Obstetrics at Ayrshire Central Hospital in Irvine, he was a true innovator, even hypnotizing some of his patients for their surgery. Margery would tell me she remained awake for her C-section, which she said was done under local anesthesia. When I was a medical student who knew everything, I scoffed when she told me this . Everyone knew that you couldn't have a C-section under local. It was only when I later read a history of the obstetrics unit that I discovered that Dr. DeSoldenhoff did perform C-sections under local. My mother had been right all along. I should have known.

I received her last birthday phone call with the recitation of natal events on my forty-seventh birthday. My mum died two days before my forty-eighth. It was a good way to go. She was 91 and had outlived my father.

By then living in Westbank, the nursing home on Titchfield Road, Mum had asked the attendant for a cup of tea that morning. When the attendant returned a few minutes later, Mum had gone. Very quick. There may have been a moment of chest pain; she may have reached for her nitro; we'll never know. She died surrounded by her paintings, acrylic and watercolor landscapes. She took up painting in her seventies, "Everyone needs a hobby." I have the paintings now, her landscape of daffodils in a bedroom, her study of a wicker chair in the dining room, and her watercolors of poppies in the office. She had a distinctive style—broad brushstrokes and an almost primitive look. I love her paintings.

On that fiftieth birthday, I slipped my arms through the sleeves and put on the jacket. It felt comfortable, familiar. In my cocoon of Grenfell fabric (by appointment to her Majesty), it felt like a hug—my fiftieth birthday hug—from my mum.

In my mind I heard, "Happy Birthday my child. Do you know what I was doing fifty years ago today?" I thought back to her enviably slender ankles, ankles like Mistinguett's—the greatest dancer in the world—and smiled as my hands smoothed the fabric.

That Dog Cost Twenty Guineas

"He's a bit small, isn't he?" I asked. We were at Mary Frew's house looking at their poodle Cindy Loo suckling her litter. Her most diminutive offspring took up the rear, left to suck hind teat, while his stronger sibs lay in forward positions. They had clambered over one another, jostling for location, a lot of paws-in-the-face to gain supremacy.

"He's sweet, though," countered Mother. "What a face." She knelt down to pet mother and pups; Cindy Loo arched her head back to lick Mum's hand. "What a good mother you are," Mum cooed. "All your babies are so beautiful. You must be so proud of them." Cindy Loo's pom-pom tail thumped in her dog bed, as she ignored the food frenzy going on around her soft underbelly. Mother had the opinion that all babies were cute. She even loved baby wood storks, and wood storks are some of the ugliest birds on the planet, with faces only a mother wood stork could love.

Lucy, the snow-white Persian, sauntered in regally and pressed the length of her body against Mum's calves, curving her back. "And you're beautiful too, Lucy." She didn't want any household member to have her feelings hurt. I hadn't realized until then that Margery was a dog person. I had always assumed she was a cat person since Ming, our blind Siamese, ruled the roost at home. Ming stalked the birds in the back garden, hunting by sound and vibration. To give the birds ample warning of Ming's whereabouts, since Mum could not bear the thought of her actually catching one, she sported a bell; her jangling gave the avians ample time to take wing.

Over the next few weeks the littermates were sold and, after weaning, left for their new homes. Apart from one, that is. Only mister suck-at-the-back was left. And so it was that within a few months Pepe Loo Fandango Radford moved down the crescent from number one to number seventeen.

Mary had been very persuasive. Mum negotiated a price. Dad was reticent at first, concerned about dog hair clinging to his best suits. However, he came to love him, too—Pepe didn't shed, and over time Pepe matured and grew into his role as an incredibly intelligent, easily trained toy poodle.

Before long, we found out Pepe had a delicate stomach, so delicate he could not have off-the-shelf dog food, so Margery provided customized meals. One day when I came home from school, she was in the kitchen, steam rising from the pan in front of her. The stench immediately hit me like a wall; my eyes stung. "What's that dreadful smell?"

"I'm boiling a beef heart for Pepe," she replied, in a matter-of-fact way, as if boiling a beef heart were an everyday occurrence.

I can tell you, there is nothing like the stink of a beef heart on the stove. Except perhaps that of a beef tongue boiling; that's a close second. Then, of course, there's haggis, the ultimate concoction of organ meat— heart, liver, and tongue—all boiled together, ground and squeezed into a sheep's stomach. Yummy.

How did she even think of cooking Pepe beef heart? Did the butcher on Portland Street suggest it one day when she was purchasing pork chops? I can imagine him wrapping the chops in white paper and her mentioning the finicky dog and his hard-to-please intestines. Then, "I've some beef hearts in the back, Mrs. Radford. He may like those," and parceling them up, too, wiping his hands on his white-but-bloodied butcher's apron as he beamed under his white trilby.

Sometimes Margery prepared mince—hamburger—in gravy. I don't remember our own dinners getting quite as much attention. Once I made the mistake of complaining about the Bird's Eye fish fingers for dinner and was promptly thrown out of the house, a fifty pence piece pressed into my hand, and told to go find my own dinner. After a walk around Troon I soon discovered 50p bought slim pickings. I appreciated fish fingers after that experience. And perhaps if a home-cooked meal meant beef heart, Bird's Eye wasn't so bad.

The first time Pepe had to go to the groomer, it prompted a family conference about the kind of cut he should have. As the antithesis of a show dog—being the runt of the litter and all—a Lion Cut seemed a bit grandiose. We didn't want our dog viewed as a social climber, either. We settled on a lamb cut—a little bouffant on his head, close-cropped on the body, thicker on the legs, with a pom-pom tail. He had tiny, delicate feet, and clipped nails. When the wind came off the Atlantic, though, that scant curly coat of his didn't keep him warm, and he'd return shivering from his walks on Troon promenade.

"Chilly, lad?" Dad inquired of the dog on one occasion. Pepe turned his head sideways, listening intently. "You need a coat." Being a bespoke tailor, making Pepe a coat was a simple task for Sidney. First he had to be measured, a soft tape measure brought round his chest and hips. Then Dad drew out a pattern on brown tailor's paper, out of which he fashioned the patterns for his gentlemen's suits. This first pattern, housed in a section of his workshop, served as the template for all subsequent coats. My favorite garment was a little number in light blue Thompson tartan with a scarlet satin lining and a short collar that covered the back of Pepe's neck. The coat had an attached belt, not only stylish but also functional, winding under his soft belly and buttoning on his back to secure the coat in place. Très chic pour monsieur Pepe.

Often, I would take him on the sand dunes on the way to the beach. The grass was long enough that all I could see would be his little pom-pom tail above the grass.

Pepe suffered from chronic constipation, perhaps caused by a diet of rich meat and no fiber. Mum would get irritated and complain, "That dog cost twenty guineas and he's sickly."

Once I pointed out that—amortized over the life of the animal—it was only pennies a day. I received "the look" for that one.

One evening during my early years of medical school, someone came to fetch me from the dorm library. Mum was on the phone. "Pepe was put to sleep today. Your Dad can't stop crying." Pepe was seventeen.

I still miss his little pom-pom tail. In a drawer of my bedside table I keep some special items. There, next to my dad's sable hairbrush, is the tag from Pepe's collar. It doesn't have his name, only our phone number, engraved by hand in a shaky script: Troon 592. I also still have a lock of his hair in an envelope, taken from one of his lamb cuts. Yes, he cost twenty guineas, but he was priceless.

The Kittens Are in the Oven Under a Low Gas

I cycled my bike as fast as it would go, legs pumping, pedals spinning free at the bottom of the hill, eyes tearing, ears buzzing, racing to Auntie Mary's at lunch time for the arrival of the kittens. Lucy, the Frew's over-bred, pure, superior Persian had been "fulfilled" by the local tomcat. While my mother and Mary both believed that animals should be fulfilled, I favored neutering, myself. Come to think of it, Pepe was neutered, so Mum's opinion on "fixing" was, apparently, variable.

Lucy was, indeed, gorgeous, sleek (except while pregnant), elegant, aloof, yet, at the same time, dumb as two short planks and devoid of essential maternal instincts. I careened round the corner to the back door, abandoned the bike, and blasted into the neighbors' warm, comfy kitchen, panting, my school uniform blazer falling off-the-shoulder. I saw Lucy in a makeshift bed in a corner, looking tired, disinterested, preening her snow-white fur, but without vigor. I saw no kittens.

"Where are they?" I asked.

"They're in the oven under a low gas."

Shocked, I swiveled my head to the open oven door. There, on a cookie sheet on a middle shelf, were four little balls, one pure black, fur still damp, their eyes tightly shut. We gently took them out and rubbed them softly. They stirred in response.

Mum told me the saga over a cup of tea, cozied up around the kitchen table, under a print of an Impressionist painting of the circus (a ringmaster directs a festooned lady atop a big-rumped horse). Mum had been called into service as Lucy's midwife when it was apparent that she was the only one available when Lucy went into labor. Mum saw early on that Lucy was

11

Diane Radford

clueless: after the first kitten emerged, covered in the thin membrane that was the amniotic sac, Lucy made no attempt to remove the cowl, which must be torn away in order for the kitten to breathe. Mum had to free the kitten's head and gently rub it to stimulate a breath.

"So where was Lily Murphy in all of this?" I asked referring to the town's wonderful vet, a caring soul.

"Emergency surgery. She couldn't be in two places at once."

Before she began operating on her patient at the practice, she had guided Mum by phone, even giving her the cooking instructions for drying off the little bundles.

All four survived. Mary and Al kept the black one, which they called Topsy because she "grew like Topsy," while they gave away her brothers and sister. Topsy lived a long life, yet I suspect they neutered her at the appropriate time, one delivery adventure enough for any family.

12

We've Arrived, and to Prove it, We're Here

Many children have abandonment issues—here's where mine came from.

I am a seasoned traveler, Margery and Sid taking me with them on jaunts starting when I was just a tot. On arrival at our destination, Mum would plop the suitcases on the bed, fling wide the curtains, and proclaim, "We've arrived, and to prove, it we're here." The announcement heralded the beginning of another fun-filled vacation by the sea. Yet, it was the journey to the sandy-beached spot that was sometimes fraught with adventure. So it was in the summer of 1963, when I was five.

The beaches of Normandy and Brittany beckoned, famous because of their historic D-Day import and their long stretches of white sand. The boot of the Humber Sceptre packed with bulging suitcases, we headed south for Concarneu, via the ferry at Dover, a four hundred mile drive.

Once we arrived at Dover, and were waiting in line for the ferry, my parents, both smokers in those days, decided to go to the duty-free shop to get a few cartons of cigarettes, leaving me in the car. In retrospect, I'm sure they regretted this decision soon afterwards. Within minutes, the column of cars began to creep aboard, and soon the Sceptre blocked the way. Drivers started to toot their horns. Other irate motorists shook their fists at me, which was pointless because, at five, what could I do?

What seemed to me to be hours passed. Maybe only ten minutes, but by that time I had sobbed and had no more tears and no voice. When my parents did return, with their armfuls of booze and filtered Embassies, a red-faced blubbery creature greeted them. They were in deep trouble, and they knew it. Even my lavender plush elephant could not console me.

Fortunately, the ferry had not left the dock. Dad took the controls and steered us aboard, the last car on the ferry.

Despite the trauma, we made it to our destination safe and sound, and Mum was able to announce, "We've arrived, and to prove it, we're here." But we nearly didn't arrive and almost weren't there. The near miss haunts me to this day.

So if you're traveling with me and decide to just drop in to the duty-free for a moment, expect me to blanch a little as I grip your sleeve.

Have a Chitter-Bite

The beaches at Troon have been renowned for decades. A railway poster from the 1920s depicts a long-skirted lady golfer finishing her swing, the beach stretching out behind her and yachts traversing the bay. It reads, "Troon, Ideal Holiday Resort. Six golf courses, sandy beach, boating, bathing, tennis, bowling and other attractions." And at the bottom, "The Golf Courses on the West Coast of Scotland are most conveniently reached by the Midland & Glasgow & South Western Railways." I have often commented about Troon that, with a population of around 13,000, the ratio of golf courses to people sounds just about right to me.

Divided by the point—Truin—where the harbor and ship works are located, the North beach and South beach together make up seven miles of sandy shore. Looking across the bay, the Christmas pudding-shaped island Ailsa Craig (a bird sanctuary) lies to the south; low-lying Lady Isle and its larger backdrop, Arran, to the North. Goat Fell rises to the highest point on Arran, the contour of the mountainous backbone of the island forming the well-recognized "Sleeping Warrior." Living closer to the South beach, that bay was our most popular haunt, whether for walking the dog or for a dip in the surf in July.

Summer on the west coast of Scotland is a capricious, transient season. The sky can be robin's egg blue, with the clouds cottony and puffy, only to transform in minutes into a grey, ominous scene, accompanied by gale-force winds which whip the sand from the dunes.

On one of the many days in between these two extremes, Mother gathered up the accoutrements for a day at the beach and mustered the troops, six-year-old me and Pepe the poodle. Among the required equipment for us and other beachcombers was the windbreak, a long canvas sheet strung on wooden poles, in the lee of which we changed,

15

spread out our towels, picnicked, and, from its shelter, scurried down to the water's edge. Essential, too, was the mallet to fix it in place. Horizontally striped and colorful, as if to brighten up their true purpose, windbreaks can be seen still, in action, on Troon beach.

Mum's biceps tensed as she grabbed the mallet. She swung vigorously, and a metallic twang rang out when she made contact with the covered tip of the stake. "Stand back, family," she cried, heaving the tool for another swing. Pepe and I backed off to a safe distance. A few more swift arcs in the air and the windbreak was secure. In between its constraints, it billowed like a sail. Margery spread out our towels, then reached for the thermos. She unscrewed the top and I caught the aroma of tea and another more bitter scent that I would recognize later to be whisky. She took a gulp. "Ahhhhh." She poured me an Orangina.

We paused and observed the scenes along the beach. Windbreaks were dotted up and down the sand, families forming their own little outposts close enough to the water's edge. Further along the beach were the pony rides, where children's legs stuck out at awkward angles atop the rounded girth of the Shetland ponies. Togneri's ice cream van was parked on the esplanade, serving twisty soft cones and 99s, the vanilla cone with a Cadbury flake stuck in it.

"All right, Lass, time to change." Mother pulled her changing shroud out of the carryall, a voluminous garment Dad had tailored to enable her to change into and out of her suit without having to do a potentially embarrassing dance involving towels, wet suits, and underwear. He fashioned it out of terry cloth with a blue and green large floral print, complete with a drawstring around the neck and, when pulled, Mum's head was the only part of her exposed. I saw lots of movement going on underneath, until eventually, she emerged in her ruched suit. She then donned her petaled rubber swim cap and plastic buckled water shoes. I was too small to be able to make use of the personal changing tent, and so had to perform the towel dance, which generally left me with sand in my bathing costume or my knickers. Once properly attired, we headed off down the sands to the awaiting ocean.

In our scurry to the sea we dodged sharp shells, crinkly seaweed, and moribund jellyfish. The first toe in the water felt shriekingly cold, but I quickly got used to it. Paddling first, gauging the temperature, I sensed the surface of shells beneath, and then plunged in, every inch of skin underwater colder than the next. Quickly, I breaststroked against the surf, seaweed slapping me.

Mum swam a few strokes parallel to the waves and then stood up in the shallow water. "I'm going back in, pet," she cried. "I'll watch you from the windbreak."

I emerged from the sea fifteen minutes later, blue-lipped and shivering, dripping rivulets down my goose-skin legs as I ran back up the sands. Mother met me halfway, unwrapping a Tunnocks caramel wafer. She proffered it, bending towards me, "Have a chitter-bite, my love." Chitter-bite was my Mother's word for any sweet treat that stopped my shivering jaws rattling against one another. The chocolate and caramel concoction left brown sticky blobs on my insensate lips. Of course, she had a chitter-bite, too, since she had become chilly watching me flounder about in the waves.

And off we walked back to our windbreak nest and her spiked thermos.

The Animal Must Roam Free

Mother played the piano with great gusto but, most people would agree, not much finesse. The upright instrument occupied a place against a wall in a small room in the front of the house in Hunter Crescent. Formerly a bedroom, when we expanded the attic, it became the music room and hamster gym. Hammy the golden hamster had a cage the color of a robin's egg and a wheel that almost satisfied his desire for exercise. Late at night, I'd hear the wheel spinning as he ran and ran and ran, his cheeks bulging with sunflower seeds.

Margery decided Hammy needed to be free to roam about the room, that however much running he did on his wheel, it could not compare to the freedom of being out of his cage. Sidney wasn't so sure. "He must be free," she threw her arms wide expansively, her pearls bouncing as her chest heaved, "He must be fulfilled. How would you like it if you were in a cage all day?" By fulfilled, on this occasion, she meant free to roam—a free-range hamster.

Dad shuffled his feet, intently studying the nap of the carpet.

Mother prevailed.

So, of an evening, out of his cage he would scamper about, while mother hammered out selections of her favorite tunes—by Lerner and Loewe if we'd just seen *My Fair Lady,* or excepts from the score of *The Sound of Music.* We typically saw movies at the Odeon in Ayr, where at intermission attendants in frilly pinnies served tiny ice cream cups and Kia-Oras complete with straws from lighted trays. It was likely the pounding on the ivories plus the vigorous pumping of the pedals, her stilettos acting like fulcrums, that prevented her hearing the rasping sound of rodent incisors at work on the carpet. Liking his change of scenery, Hammy started to chew in earnest, since he had the teeth for it.

At first there were just a few straggly strands of carpet around the pipe of the radiator. These were easily overlooked and put down to fraying. The diminutive piles of sawdust that emerged as he nibbled through the floorboards *should* have garnered our attention. Instead, one evening I went in to the piano room to put him back in his cage and found the hole in the floorboards to be a little larger, just big enough for a skinny little rodent to find his way into the foundations of the house. There are no basements in the UK, so he was under the house, in the labyrinth of water pipes and 2 x 2s.

All three of us gathered, looking at the exit hole. "It's like *The Great Escape*," said Dad, referring to the movie, "only he didn't have trousers to hide the sand." Mother glared, "Well, bright spark, what are you going to do about it? Don't just stand there; do something."

Dad stroked his chin, and after a pause, said, "We could re-name him Houdini."

"Fat lot of good that'll do." She stamped her foot.

I had a thought. In the hall coat closet, there was a removable hatch in the floor through which one could access the foundation. I grabbed his cage from its stand, ran over to the closet, shimmied on my tummy under the coats, and opened the hatch. The aperture was just the right size through which to slide the cage, his bowl laden with seeds for bait. And then we waited.

We waited and watched every hour. No hamster.

At midnight we took a final look as I beamed my torch into the hole. The circle of light illuminated an empty cage. Tears welled as I contemplated the future without the incessant, yet comforting, sound of his spinning wheel. Dad put his arm around me, squeezing a hug, "It's all right poppet, he's roaming free, as your mother would say, and he's fulfilled."

I was not consoled.

"Come on, my sweet, let's put you to bed."

Sleep was fitful as I dreamt about the poor lonely creature under the house. I wondered if there were any other rodents he could befriend down there, maybe a mouse or two.

In the morning I pulled dressing gown over pajamas and slid on my Pirelli slippers with the rubber soles that gave me better traction to sprint down the hall to the closet. Before I reached it, I heard the sound, the familiar rattle of a wheel going round and round.

I took the stairs in twos to reach my parents' bedroom.

"Hammy's come home. He's not dead. He's alive! He's alive!"

Returning to the closet, I wiggled commando style under the coats again and heaved the cage up through the floor. There he was, cheeks stuffed, running and running in his wheel. My parents hugged behind me.

"Brilliant, brilliant," exclaimed Dad. "He lives on." He pursed his lips and imitated the theme from *The Great Escape*, bazooka-style.

I carried the now-inhabited cage back to its proper place.

We looked at the semicircular cut Hammy had chewed in the carpet and floor around the radiator pipe. "Well, I guess he can't run about in this room for a while," said Mum.

Dad's eyes narrowed. "You're not thinking of letting him out again anywhere, are you? As it is, I have to call Lunardi the joiner on Academy Street to come and fix the floorboards."

She held him in a penetrating gaze. "Sidney," she paused for effect, "Sidney, the animal must be fulfilled."

Next day, our hamster ran around in the living room while I hid behind the crimson couch; *Dr. Who* was on the telly. Hammy came over to me and we crouched together, avoiding the lethal exterminator beams from the mechanical tank-like Daleks (Dr. Who's robotic nemesis).

Out of the corner of my eye I noticed a strand of carpet by the radiator had begun to unravel.

A Golden Treasury of Verse

There is almost nowhere in Troon that one is not reminded of the importance of the 4th Duke of Portland and his family and descendents to the formation and growth of the town. The Duke was responsible for the dredging of the harbor, the railway line from Glasgow, and the shipyards. His family and their names are immortalized in the public places and street names—Portland Street, Portland Church, Welbeck Crescent (after the family's estate in England), Lady Margaret Drive, Ottoline Drive, Bentinck Drive, and Cavendish Place.

It was along some of these streets that my next door neighbor William and I planned our route for Halloween in 1965. William was Batman to my Robin. We prepared for months, making Batman's distinctive belt from multiple boxes of Embassy brand cigarettes. The classic box shape with its flip top lid perfected his costume. I fastidiously painted each one gold using paint from model airplane kits and a sable brush; William persuaded all the smokers we knew to inhale Embassy brand and not toss out the containers. It took more than ten gilded boxes to complete the look.

Dad fashioned the red satin fabric that had served as the lining for Pepe the poodle's tartan coat into the distinctive cape for my Robin costume. We looked fabulous. Even Adam West would have been proud. No Batmobile, however; we used Shanks's pony for transport; in other words, we walked.

In Scotland, as in the rest of the UK, the costumed child is expected to perform in order to receive her goodies. Guising (children dressing up in disguise and going round the neighborhood) has taken place in Scotland since the late 1800s. No 'Trick or Treat" here; rather "Trick, then Treat." Children perform their "party-piece" before being rewarded with coins, confections, even cuddles. William had a joke ready, a pretty good one-liner. Poring through mother's *Golden Treasury of Verse*, I decided to recite Longfellow's "Hiawatha."

I made my announcement to Mum in the kitchen where the pressure cooker hissed in an alarming way as usual. I always feared that contraption, thinking it would blow us all up.

"You're going to recite what?" she asked as she spun around from the stove.

"'Hiawatha,'" I repeated, "by Longfellow."

"But Pet, it's so long. Twenty-two chapters. How many stanzas are you planning?"

This question stymied me, for I just presumed that the listeners would hang onto every word of 5,314 lines.

"As many as I can remember."

She opened the cooker and steam shot forth. Turning back to me, her glasses fogged, she said, "May I suggest an abridged version? People will have no mind to stand in a open doorway listening to you prattle on, however charmingly you prattle."

She had a point. It would be drafty.

I rehearsed for days until I committed my selected verses to memory.

On the not-too-chilly night in October, William and I set out—resplendent in our attire—the dynamic duo in miniature, capes wafting behind us as we walked down Hunter Crescent to Ottoline Drive (named after Ottoline Bentinck, the half sister of William Cavendish Bentinck, the 5th Duke of Portland). At least we would visit familiar territory—the Begbies, the Cooks, the Mackays—on our route.

At our first stop, William chapped on the door with his gauntleted knuckles, yelled "Halloween" as the door opened, and quickly told his joke. Our gracious neighbor wiped her hands on her pinny, reached behind her, and dropped an apple in his plastic bag. Then it was my turn. I took a breath and began,

> By the shores of Gitche Gumee,
> By the shining Big-Sea-Water,
> Stood the wigwam of Nokomis,
> Daughter of the Moon, Nokomis.

When I said water, I added a little ripple-like hand gesture for effect. Mrs. Begbie reached for another apple, thinking my recital done. She plopped it in the bag. I took this as a sign she enjoyed trochaic tetrameter, and I resumed.

> Dark behind it rose the forest,
> Rose the black and gloomy pine-trees,
> Rose the firs with cones upon them;
> Bright before it beat the water...

Her eyes narrowed as she tossed in some caramels and a shiny sixpence. She's really a poetry lover, I thought. I carried on.

> Beat the clear and sunny water,
> Beat the shining Big-Sea-Water.

She started to close the door. I asked if she'd like to hear another verse. She opened her purse, turned it upside down, and all the spare change fell into my bag. "No, dear." The door shut.

I turned to William, "I think she liked it."

We carried on to Lady Margaret Drive (named after Lady Margaret Bentinck, the Duchess of Portland and wife of the 2nd Duke of Portland, and mother of William the 3rd Duke) and repeated our skits to the Lewises. By the time we turned back onto Hunter Crescent after visiting the Frews, the Thompsons, and the Holmeses, our bags were laden. Our best reception was at the Walkers. Jimmy was an English teacher at Kilmarnock Academy, a great lover of literature, and he could doubtless have recited many a verse himself.

Once home, I displayed my stash to Mum and told her about the upturned purse and the doors closing.

"Good thing you were wearing a mask. What are you going to try next year?"

"I thought perhaps 'The Charge of the Light Brigade'." I brandished an imaginary saber for emphasis. "There are only six verses."

She thought for a moment, "You know, Dorothy Parker has a very short poem—'You Might as Well Live'—about suicide. You may want to

23

try that, or our poor neighbors may, indeed, be contemplating their own demise." She shook her head, "Death by poetry; God love us."

And with that she helped me out of my tights—saying "skin a rabbit" as she did so—and sent me off to bed.

Reading Love Letters

In our house, as in households across the UK, the day before Ash Wednesday—Shrove Tuesday—was the day of the evening pancake feast. Shrove Tuesday is observed in several Christian denominations, including ours, the Episcopal Church. The term "shrove" is derived from the word "shrive," meaning to confess. It is a day of reflection, before the penitential season of Lent.

Historically, Shrove Tuesday (also celebrated as Mardi Gras or Fat Tuesday) is the day to use up foods that would be sacrificed during the fasting or relative scarcity of Lent, foods such as flour, milk, and eggs, which also happen to be the ideal ingredients for pancake or crêpe batter.

Margery Radford was a skilled crêpe-crafter. I'd observe the ritual from a corner of our kitchen in Hunter Crescent. She sifted the flour and salt into the bowl, and then created a small well in the center into which she cracked an egg. After some intense whisking, she let the batter rest while we set the table together. We were a team—she carried the placemats and crockery while I followed behind with the cutlery.

And then the magic of crêpe creation began. After pouring the batter into the hot frying pan, she deftly tipped it, spreading the paper-thin layer evenly over the base. Mum turned to me and asked, "Know how thin these crêpes should be, pet?" I shook my head no.

"So thin you could read your love letters through them," she declared, nodding for emphasis, and with that flipped the crêpe with a brisk movement. Now that's really thin, I thought to myself.

After half a dozen crêpes had been arranged on three plates, Mum gently tapped the sieve containing the powdered sugar, dusting each one. She cupped her left hand over her right as she finished the dish with lemon juice and carried her culinary creation over to the kitchen table where Dad was waiting expectantly. "Ah," said Dad, "another perfect plate of pancakes."

So perfect, you could read your love letters through them.

I'm Taking Some Brandy
to the Guinea Pigs

I once asked Margery why a bungalow was called a bungalow. She turned her head to me, pondered a moment, and announced triumphantly, "They built one floor, and then they bunged a low roof on it." That satisfied me well enough, although I later learned the word has origins in India and was used to describe the dwellings of the sailors of the East India Company, and then the houses of the British Raj officials. To describe our small home on Hunter Crescent as a bungalow connotes a rather unwarranted colonial exoticism. Despite its humbleness, to me it has always been the best house, for it is the first one I remember.

Passers-by standing on the pavement or sidewalk, looking toward the house, would see two large rosebeds, a huge semicircular bed in front and a smaller lunar shaped one to the left. Margery planted, tended, pruned, fertilized, and adored her roses. With just four feet separating it from the bungalow, to the left of the house stood the detached pebble-dashed garage, and inside, leaning against the back wall, was the hutch in which nestled the guinea pigs, Toffee and Muffin.

All Radford animals were special, and these were exceptional guinea pigs. Toffee, as the name suggests, was all brown; Muffin more of a skewbald variety with brown and white blotches. If he'd been a horse, he would have been a pinto. The base of the hutch was covered in straw purchased from Crossburn, the Collins' farm located in Loans, the village over the burn and up the road a bit. Lacking heat, the garage seemed to shiver in winter, and Toffee and Muffin would have too, had Margery not come to the rescue, placing a blanket over the hutch and bearing a libation "to warm the cockles of their hearts."

So there we would be in the living room on a winter evening, Mother having sipped her sherry and me with my cowboy suit on as we watched *Rawhide* starring a young Clint Eastwood. At some point, Mum would say, "Chilly out. I'm taking some brandy to the guinea pigs," as if it were the most natural thing in the world. And off she'd trot bearing a thimbleful of Courvoisier out to the garage, shielding it with a cupped hand from the wind.

Whether the small servings ever made it to the garage or not is unclear. It's possible they were consumed by the bearer along the journey. Brandy or no brandy, Toffee and Muffin appeared happy in their abode, though it could be they were pleasantly pickled.

There's a Grave Danger You'll Live

The horses' field at the end of Hunter Crescent in Troon, beside the Frew's bungalow at number one, was about two acres. I remember that at least. The field has been built upon since then; a subdivision of red brick houses covers the ground on which Aga, the Appaloosa, once grazed. One year, a smaller rotund bay pony, which went by the innocuous name of Muffin, visited temporarily. He was an amiable steed, his round belly resembling those penned by cartoonists. Our friends the Martins lived across the road from the field in the elegant white Dunchattan mansion, protected by tall pines and reached by a winding driveway. Behind the house, further into the woods, were some gaily painted jumps on a well-trodden path.

It is said girls go through three phases as they develop into adolescence: dolls, then horses, then boys. I went straight to the horse phase (unless you count GI Joe as a doll). My parents treated me to lessons at the militaristic Wright's Riding Academy, housed in the stables of the Fullarton Mansion. The house, itself, had been demolished several years earlier in 1962, but I still recall its imposing façade.

The environment at the academy was "structured," commanded by Mr. Wilson, who donned an epauletted black riding jacket and often rode the grand, handsome palomino El Dorado. We Academy students wore a school uniform: white shirt, black tie, and black sweater for mucking out and cleaning tack; black riding jacket or tweed hacking jacket for riding. In these days it seemed I was always in uniform. During the school week, I donned a blazer, the breast pocket bearing the school crest, paired with the obligatory grey skirt, and long white socks, and on weekends, I sported my Wright's Riding Academy uniform.

There were some great ponies at the Academy: Trixie, Shamrock, Comanche, and Smartie. The stables stood across the driveway from Marr

Rugby Clubhouse and playing fields. When the stables were converted to townhouses and flats, the Academy moved further into Southwoods, an area known for its imposing, expensive mansions sequestered behind high walls.

The rest of this story, or at least the action part of it, I have reconstructed from what I've been told, for my memory of the event was erased by the injury. My friend (a relative of the Martins) and I were permitted to saddle up two ponies, one being Muffin, and trot off to the jumps. According to my mum, we had a fun afternoon, clearing the jumps and cantering along the path. Until, that is, I "lost my knees" and crashed precipitously onto the forest floor, striking my head on a log. Mr. Wilson, had he been there, would have been dismayed by my lack of skill.

I don't know how long I remained unconscious, but someone hoisted me up and carried me home to terrified parents, who put me to bed. In the retellings, no mention was ever made of my being taken to the accident and emergency department of the hospital; rather, our GPs (either Dr. McPhee or Dr. Macintosh) visited daily to check on my concussion, as house calls were part of their usual care. The story goes that I vomited often. As the days passed, I gradually noticed the design on the flowery wallpaper and heard the occasional engine noise as a car tooled along the crescent. While I wore a hard hat to ride, in those days the velvet-covered riding helmets with the ribbon on the back were more ornamental that functional. Modern riding helmets have at least some semblance of protection from head trauma. The head for which Mrs. Martin had knitted an angora wool pink-and-white bonnet as a gift at my birth, using an orange as a model, was barely protected by my sartorially-correct riding hat.

My memory begins about five days after the accident. The concussion, my subsequent medical school training would teach me, had caused retrograde amnesia (a condition in which recent past events cannot be remembered). By that point though, I was improving. In fact, Mother declared, "You can go back to school on Monday."

School, school...her words filtered through to recognition. Monday. Monday. My grey matter cells buzzed to attention. Something about Monday. I thought about the upcoming week at school. The injured synapses fired, conveying my shock to my tongue. "Monday," I wailed, "I can't go back Monday. I have a French exam. Could you consider

Tuesday?" How could I be expected to craft sentences in a foreign language so soon after this life-threatening event? Negotiation was to no avail. I was sunk, my goose was cooked. Mon oie a été cuit.

Turning on her heel, Mum announced, "You'll just have to thole it, my little choufleur," reverting to her North-of-England roots for that statement. It was one of her quirky Margeryisms, meaning I'd just have to put up with it. She traipsed down the corridor singing, "Three little girls from school are we," dancing a little fancy footwork as she went, right hand spiraling in the air.

Marr College, the local high school, put on a Gilbert and Sullivan operetta every year, and that year, it had been the classic *The Mikado,* set in Japan. Ever since we'd had the family outing to see the show (which, I have to add, was fabulous) Mother had been singing a medley of G and S hits as she went about her household chores. She'd lustily sing out "I Have a Little List," "A Wandering Minstrel I," and "The Moon and I." For "Behold the Lord High Executioner," she'd add the snapping movement of an imaginary fan shutting. To this day, that production of *The Mikado* is the pinnacle to which I hold all other productions. The D'Oyly Carte Company once came to St. Louis on tour and almost met the standard of the Marr College Players… almost.

As Mum reached the kitchen at the other end of the house, she yelled, "There's a grave danger you'll live, madam." And that was that—a final pronouncement. She was in a take no prisoners mood. I attended school on Monday.

Contrary to my pessimistic predictions, my academic career did not end that Monday. I was tested. I passed. Life went on. The exam was a piece of cake, un morceau de gateaux.

I have capitalized on the cranial catastrophe, however, in the years hence, during which I trained as a cancer surgeon specializing in breast cancer. On meeting an electrical engineer, I've been known to jest, "I could have been an electrical engineer if I hadn't had that head injury." And, yes, I've inserted many a profession into that phrase for a cheap chuckle.

I suppose Mum would be proud of my bon mots, though if it were her quip, I'm sure she'd work in a song and dance routine to boot.

Part Two

Bentinck Drive

Our home on Bentinck Drive was red sandstone and pebble-dash and stood not far from the corner of Yorke Road. Mother called it Abernyte, and Dad had to hang a sign with that name on the front of the house. It sounded awfully grand, and, indeed, it was bigger than our house on Hunter Crescent. The detached two-car garage was entered via a lane between Bentinck Drive and South Beach, which was one street closer to the beach. Along the path connecting the garage with the back door were two brick outbuildings, one used for tools and one for the large chest freezer.

The family room to the rear of the house exited onto a paved patio, beyond which, on the northwest side, was a greenhouse. Just as on Hunter Crescent, Margery planted rose beds. A crabapple tree bore fruit annually from which Margery would make jam. My room was upstairs and to the front of the house, where Pepe, my ever-faithful canine companion, would come sleep with me at night. We moved to Bentinck Drive soon after I started at Marr College, eleven going on twelve years old.

One of the best features of this house was its proximity to the beach. Turning right onto Yorke Road and right again onto South Beach by the South Beach Hotel, we then had only a few yards across the road to the cutout leading to the promenade and the dunes. Perfect for walking the dog, or an evening's "constitutional."

We were all three golfers, and the golf courses of Old Troon and Troon Ladies' Golf Club were half a mile away. Often, Dad would walk to the course, pulling his clubs behind, bent at the waist to counter the gusting wind.

Worse Things Happen At Sea

Every year, after months of hard work my parents rewarded themselves with a holiday, often overseas. One of their favorite destinations was the Costa Brava on the northeast coast of Spain. Before any of her excursions abroad, Margery felt it her bounden duty to learn the local lingo and play with the pitter-patter of the patois. She had sets of LPs organized beside the teak RCA gramophone in the living room: Parliamo Italiano for their vacation to Venice; French by Berlitz for the Parisian adventure; and Berlitz again for Spanish. For weeks before our Thomson all-inclusive holiday to the beaches of L'Estartit in Catalonia, she sequestered herself in an armchair, vocabulary guide open, trying to master this romance language. On the morning of departure, as we left the house for the drive to Glasgow Airport, she slipped her Spanish phrase book into a capacious white handbag. "En avant," she waved at the open road, urging Dad to drive faster, lapsing into French, a more familiar tongue to her.

"Shouldn't it be ándale, ándale?" I chimed in from the back seat, cracking an imaginary whip.

"Whatever, you get my drift. Off we go. The Radfords on vacation." Dad sank the pedal—ever lead-footed—and we sped to Abbotsinch to catch our plane.

Our first few days at the Flamingo Hotel were spent on the sands or by the pool. Evenings were filled with aromatic paella, the staccato of flamenco dancers, and I recall an image of sangria being poured into my mother's open mouth from an ascending porrón held by an amused waiter. A gypsy came by daily with her dancing monkey, which hopped from foot to foot and twirled to her beat on the ribboned tambourine.

One morning Margery announced, "Enough of this endless stream of merriment, my dear family. It's time to learn some history of the area." She pointed to the list of excursions on the notice board in the lobby. Her hand waved at a heading. "The Roman Ruins of Ampurias. That should satisfy our need for culture." Always the educator, Mum had long ago decided I should share her lifelong lust for learning: she signed us up. Meanwhile, Dad felt quite cultured enough, thank you, and chose to stay poolside with a detective novel.

The coach picked us up for the twelve mile drive to Ampurias, along with thirty or so other inquiring vacationers, some already red round the edges from the harsh sun, some grasping their Fodor's guide to read up on the way. Founded by the Greeks in the sixth century BC, then occupied by the Romans, the city is considered one of the most important archeological sites in Spain.

We meandered through the ancient Roman ruins, pausing to take in the magnificent view from the cliff-edge of the azure sea below. The city was orderly. "Let's go to the Ciudad," Margery intoned, pronouncing it Theeoodad.

I wiped my face with a tissue and asked, "Why are you lisping?"

"It's the Catalan pronunciation, *c* is pronounced *th*." Proof that she'd been listening to her Spanish lessons in her spare time at home.

"Yes, let's thaunter over there and thee the thea," I said, getting into the spirit.

"You're taking the Mickey, Madam."

"Thure I am."

After a few hours poring over the mosaic tile floors, checking out the statue of Aesculapius, and admiring the view from the cliffside over the choppy bay below, I had a sense of unease.

"What time does the coach leave?" I asked.

"I don't know, 2 o'clock, I think."

"Well, what time is it now?"

"I don't have a watch on."

With some anxiety, I headed over to the coach parking lot, scanning it for ours. No coach. It was gone. My hands felt clammy. I turned on my heels and ran back to the Roman ruins where Mother still studied the design on the floor.

"The coach isn't there." My voice rose. "They've gone without us."

"Don't be ridiculous, my child. They would have done a head count." Unconvinced, she strode over to the parking lot with me to see for herself, then shook her head in disbelief. "Bugger it, you're right."

Before cell phones, and with no phone booths among the ruins, it wasn't like we could just call someone up to come get us.

"Well, I guess it is time to check out your Spanish," I said. "We're going to have to ask for a lift."

There were a few other coaches in the lot, but none was going back to L'Estartit. An old pickup rumbled up the dusty, unpaved road to the parking lot. The engine shuddered to a stop, and a wiry leather-faced workman hopped out, dropping off some painting supplies to revamp one of the tourist shops. There being no one else to ask, Mum approached him. I caught a few words: Flamingo Hotel, L'Estartit. She gestured and gesticulated. The tanned, wrinkled man started to smile in comprehension. He beamed at me and proffered a hand to help me clamber onto the wheel well and into the back of the truck. He did the same for Mum, as she held the skirt of her dress down with one hand, the wind gusting it upward. Soon we were both sitting in the dusty truck bed, our backs up against the cab. Our chauffeur turned around to see we were settled. We gave him the thumbs up, and the engine grumbled into life. Mum held onto her sunhat as we took off along the circuitous road, clouds of dust pluming behind us.

"Think of this as an adventure," she yelled at me as we lurched from side to side.

"I'll write an essay about it in English class when I get back to school," said I. "No one will believe it." Part of the journey took us along the steep cliffside. Below us the froth-tipped swell hit the rocks on the shore. The truck heaved its way along the edge, the gear change jarring our ears. The sea did look beautiful, though, as we caught sight of the expanse of the bay as we rounded the corners. Mother gripped my arm to steady me, her other hand white-knuckled on the side of the truck, as my bottom slid on the slick truck bed. "My bum is really going to hurt by the time we get there," I said.

When the truck rumbled to a stop outside the hotel steps, I gingerly attempted to move. Every body part ached. Dad ran out to greet us. "What the hell happened? The coach arrived, and you weren't on it. I've been screaming bloody murder for the past hour."

Mum reached out to touch his elbow and pacify him. "Not to worry, love. It was all my fault for not watching the time." His shoulders relaxed a bit. He reached into his jacket for his wallet and offered our driver some pesetas. Our champion waved his hand no, hugged us both, and drove off.

Mum linked arms with Dad and steered him into the lobby. "Worse things happen at sea." She patted his hand. "No wrecks and nobody drownded." She took on her Lancashire accent for emphasis to add some levity.

I limped behind them, rubbing my behind. Another Radford adventure for the scrapbook.

Margery on Wheels

"I've decided to take lunches to the old folk; I'm volunteering for Meals on Wheels." Such was my mother's pronouncement one late afternoon after I had cycled home from Marr. I'd taken my usual route: up the long driveway from the school to the top of the hill, then down the embankment to the municipal golf courses, skirting the edge of the grass by the railway line. All the while my satchel, attached by an old belt of Dad's to the metal carriage on the back, flopped up and down with each bump in the terrain. Then the home stretch: down Polo Gardens to Yorke Road, over another hill bridging the railway tracks, and freewheeling down to Bentinck Drive.

"Sounds great," I panted, taking off my purple Marr blazer with gold piping on the sleeves. In the back of my mind I felt a nag of worry. Mum was never a confident driver. Nonetheless, I admired her courage to undertake a task that involved extra driving.

Off we set on a Saturday a few weeks later, meals in insulated containers piled high in the back seat and with a list of about ten stops. Bank Street proved tricky—it inclined, and hill starts were never Margery's strong point. After we'd made the delivery and she'd ensured the shut-in had his cutlery, water, napkin, and food, we climbed back in the car. Immediately, beads of sweat formed on her upper lip. A hill start is a well-timed maneuver with a stick shift, a coordination of pressure on the accelerator while easing up on the clutch and simultaneously releasing the hand brake to produce forward motion. I talked her through it, since I had seen Dad do the maneuver many times, and before long we pulled out into tarmac, and her shoulders relaxed. "Okay, onto the next stop," she announced.

I remember when Mother decided she would learn to drive; I was about four. She had a rugged determination when she set about a task—the tenacity of a terrier. Women where we lived often did not drive in those days; instead, they relied on their husbands or public transport. Her independent streak won through though, and looking back now, I believe she wanted to go back to teaching and needed to be able to transport herself since Dad worked at the shop every day.

And so began the driving lessons. Because I was not yet in school, I came along for the ride, as it were, bouncing in the back seat of the instructor's vehicle, but commanded to remain quiet. "No backseat driving from you, young lady," Mum said, swiveling to stare me in the eye for emphasis.

Mum never seemed comfortable in the driver's seat. She became easily flustered, and her hands clasped the steering wheel in a death grip. "Relax, Mrs. Radford, you don't have to pull the wheel off its housing," the instructor would say. It was a stick shift, manual transmission, Mum called it, which added to the complexity of the task at hand. Shifting gears often left me clutching my hands over my ears in the back, so awful was the grinding noise.

"Sorry," said Mum. Thinking back, it reminds me of a Bob Newhart sketch in which he plays a driving instructor—the worried, anxious tone of the teacher; the increasing pitch of the commands; the sweaty brow. Bob could have been Mum's instructor.

After a few tries, she did pass her test and came home with a driver's license, valid till she turned sixty-five. Her first car was a bubble on wheels, the dependable Morris Minor. That version in the early sixties had no indicator lights as we know them now. It had "trafficators," lit arrows about six inches long that flipped out from their position flush with the chassis to point right or left (depending on the side of the vehicle). The trafficators fascinated me, and I begged her to flip them in and out just for fun, which must have confused the drivers behind us no end.

Shortly after she passed her test, she drove to Morgenthaler's—the hairdressers on Portland Street—for her weekly shampoo and set from Mrs. Murray. Mrs. Murray cut my hair, too, with a cutthroat razor, the kind the Gorbals gangs used for maiming in *No Mean City*. So the story goes—as Alison Hollis (née Frew) recounted it to me, it was on this day of the hairdo that the yellow lines to denote parking restrictions were to be repainted in the town center, and the police had placed placards on every lamppost that noted the times to park elsewhere. Maybe Mum was so excited to have found a parking spot right outside the shop, never wondering at the empty street, or maybe she was lost in her own thoughts; whatever the reason, she was oblivious to the signs.

A couple of hours later, when she exited the shop—a vision of loveliness transformed by Wella, waving her usual goodbye to Mr. Morgenthaler and Mrs. Murray—Margery saw the car, solo on the street, around which was painted on the tarmac a four-inch wide yellow stripe. The line ran parallel to the curb, except for the boxy detour it made around the black pudgy Morris Minor. As Alison told it, Mum felt so humiliated, she abandoned the car there, rather than have someone see her get into it, walked to the bus-stop, caught the red double-decker home, and sent Sidney back later to pick up the stranded vehicle.

Sometimes she drove me to school, though most of the time I rode my bike. There were two driveways to the copper-domed high school: the one to the left to the front of the school and the sandstone steps leading to the heavy arched doorway, and the one to the right to the girls' playground and the prefabricated classrooms built in the late sixties to accommodate the expanding number of schoolchildren. I always veered right to the bike rack.

One rainy morning, Mum said, "Hop in. I'll take you today. It's raining and you'll be soaked otherwise." I happily obliged, the thought of spending the day in a wet skirt and sodden shoes unappealing. She drove an Austin by then, but still leaned forward in her usual driving posture, nervously peering through the rhythmic sweep of the windshield wipers. "I can barely see the front of the bonnet," her voice edgy.

We came upon the V-shaped intersection quite suddenly. "Right or left?"

I thought it through.

Again, this time louder, "Right or left? Hurry up, make a decision."

"Right," I yelled.

By this time she had already started to turn her wheels left, so we met the curb head on and bounced onto the rain-soaked grass.

"Bugger," she said.

"Double bugger," I said from the passenger seat.

"Don't use language like that."

"Well YOU did,"

"Never mind what I did. We may be stuck here."

She put the car in reverse, the usual crunching sound from the transmission.

The wheels spun, spitting mud onto the tree trunks ahead. We were in luck. The car inched back, and we heard a thud as the front of the car returned to the roadway.

She stared ahead of her, her chest heaving. "Your father's taking you the next time it rains."

And he did.

The General's Rooms

"Let's do it," said Mum from the passenger seat. "Let's just stop the car and just do it. It's always so much fun."

Dad looked over at her, arched an eyebrow, then nodded in agreement. "Well, Margery, for you dear, anything."

Mum belted out a few lines from the movie *Oliver*, which we had seen at the Odeon in Ayr a few weeks before. "I'd do anything, for you dear anything, for you mean everything to me. I'd go anywhere, for your smile, anywhere, for your smile everywhere I'd see."

When she got to "Go to Timbuktu," I chimed in from the back, "And back again."

Our musical interlude over, Dad eased the car to a halt on the downhill slope and put it in neutral. After a few short moments, we felt the car move—with no assistance from the driver.

"We're going backwards," Mum peered through the car window with narrowed lids, "when we should be going forwards." She swiveled around in the passenger seat to look behind her. "It never ceases to amaze me; I love this."

We were on the journey from Troon to Culzean Castle, the family home of the Kennedy Clan, a grand neo-Gothic building overlooking the bay. The serpentine road winds past where Butlin's Holiday Camp used to be and hugs the coast past the cliffs called the Heads of Ayr. Just after a bend in the road is a straight stretch that appears to be going downhill, yet, in fact, is definitely uphill. This optical illusion can be experienced by turning off the engine, putting the car in neutral, and letting the car coast.

Slowly, at first, the wheels start to roll backwards, always guaranteed to evoke oohs and aahs from the carload and a crowd-pleaser for visiting guests. You would think all that slow traffic experiencing this phenomenon would cause an accident; however, most travelers on this stretch of road know all about the Electric Brae, as it is called. It's enough to make you dizzy. Apparently it's all about the contour of the surrounding hills, the camber of the road, and the tree line. Physics may explain it, but explanation may mar the experience. It feels like magic—like electricity.

"That was grand," Dad said after we'd rolled backwards about five car lengths. "Time to get moving and see the castle." He engaged the gears, and we resumed forward momentum. Out the back window I saw there were several cars behind us that had cut their engines, too, and were rolling backwards.

Culzean Castle—pronounced Cullane, the way the name was originally spelled till Victorian times—is a masterpiece of Robert Adam architecture. Adam began his renovation of the sixteenth century tower house in 1777, a renovation that was to take over ten years and was divided into three phases. He had been commissioned by David Kennedy, the Tenth Earl of Cassillis, to create a magnificent home, a show home. And he succeeded. When first viewed from the archway at the start of the drive, the turrets and balustrades present a symmetric façade to the south. The red sandstone can take on a pinkish hue, depending on the light and time of day. In front of the castle lies the Fountain Court Garden, neatly maintained, the lawn a velvety carpet in the sunlight.

On this particular visit, one of many, not only did we plan to tour the castle and grounds, but we were also being treated to a special tour of an area not seen by many guests. Jim, the curator, was a client of Dad's—Dad tailored his bespoke suits—and he had access to parts of the house outwith the usual tour. The Kennedy family had lived in the house for generations, but in 1945 donated it and the grounds to the National Trust for Scotland.

Each room is awesome, in the old-fashioned sense of the word, in its opulence. Mother admired the damask-covered walls of the First Drawing Room and Picture Rooms. The elaborate plasterwork of cornices and centerpieces—for which Adam is renowned—is reminiscent of the designs on Wedgewood pottery. A huge mirror adorned with sphinxes sits atop the massive mantel in one of the rooms in which also hangs a painting by Alexander Nasmyth of Culzean seen from the sea, a Sheraton satinwood buffet beneath it.

Jim met us by one of the highlights of Adam's work—the oval staircase, light streaming from the cupola above to bathe the red-carpeted stairs like a spotlight. Adam exaggerated the height and grandeur of the space by placing larger, thicker, more elaborate Corinthian columns on the main floor, while the upper floor is edged with slender Ionian columns. A portrait in oils of one of the Kennedy ladies (Margaret Erskine, 1st Marchioness of Ailsa) hangs in the stairwell, her eyes and the tip of her pointed shoe appearing to follow us everywhere.

"Quite the sight," said Jim, who had walked up behind us. He indicated the sweep of the staircase. "Always a show-stopper."

"Hello, Jim. A pleasure." Dad shook his hand, and we were introduced. He took us to one of his favorite rooms to the north of the building, the one Adam named the Saloon. Oval, it overlooks the white-tipped waves of the Firth of Clyde. On this day in the late 1960s, when we were touring the room, the ceiling was white. Soon afterwards, a painting was discovered that depicts the original colors of the ceiling, pastel blues and peach tones, and it was then restored to those colors.

"What a magnificent view!" Mum spread her arms wide as she said it.

"Indeed," intoned Jim. "Adam had a vision."

Jim led us back to the behind-the-scenes elevator that took us to the flat on the upper floor called the Eisenhower Suite. When the Kennedy family donated Culzean to the National Trust in '45, it was with the proviso that a suite of rooms be given to General Eisenhower and his family to use throughout his lifetime, as a token of gratitude to the Supreme Commander Allied Expeditionary Forces in Europe in World War II. The rooms are decorated in the same grand style as the rest of the house. One sitting room faces out, overlooking the plush Fountain Court Garden. "Eisenhower would joke about this view," said Jim. "He'd say, 'Here I can stand and look out over the garden, but I have to rotate a full ninety degrees to see the Firth through the other window.'" Jim swiveled on his heels to demonstrate. After President Eisenhower died, the suite was converted to hotel rooms—with fabulous views.

Our special tour over, we headed back to the ground floor and walked the mile or so path to the Swan Pond, aptly named for its avian inhabitants complete with families of fluffy grey cygnets. In visits of later years, as age ravaged my parents' joints and balance, I'd drive the route, parking the car in one of the disabled spots by the pond, then supporting my mother by the elbow to see the birds.

Mum talked to them for a while, as she usually did with birds, assuring them they looked quite stunning in this setting. Mrs. Swan would arch her neck by way of reply. On the walk back to the car, we passed the enclosure housing the red deer, and she'd have a similar chat with the does and their fawns. Getting back in the car on one occasion, I said, "I think we should buy a house with turrets overlooking the bay."

Dad's neck reddened, "You can pay the mortgage, then."

Mum added, rolling her eyes, "What did I spawn, a social-climber?"

"I guess we'll just stay where we are," I surrendered.

When we reached the Electric Brae, of course we had to do it again. Dad took the car out of gear and his foot off the brake. We had the eerie sensation of rolling forwards while pointing uphill. In the back seat I wondered to myself whether Eisenhower ever experienced the Electric Brae. Surely someone would have shown him.

Wee Sleekit Cow'rin Tim'rous Beastie

"I think I detected a glottal stop in that statement." Margery served as the elocution police in our house—ears always attentive for a language lapse that might resemble the Scottish vernacular. If glottal were to be said with a glottal stop, it would be glo'll. Brought up in England, although she loved Scotland and lived there longer than she lived in England, no child of hers would acquire a Scottish brogue. Pure BBC, that was her goal. And there I was glottalizing inadvertently—a disgrace.

She was equally quick to pick up a dropped "th" as in "I'm going out wi' the dog."

"What did you say, Madam?" I heard, as I put Pepe's leash on and headed for the back door.

"I mean, with the dog."

"That's better."

So it was to my surprise when I came home after school one day in 1969 and told her the regional schools were having a Burns poetry reading competition that she became animated, sitting bolt upright and putting down the paper, and said "Well, you should enter it, of course."

I sighed. "But it's Burns, Mum. It's in Scots dialect."

"Of course it is, but you can do that." She had the utmost confidence in me.

Robert Burns, the National Bard of Scotland, was born on 25 January 1759 in a two room thatched cottage built by his farmer father in the village of Alloway in Ayrshire, not twelve miles from where my mother and I were talking. Burns resided there for the first seven years of his life. The surrounding Ayrshire countryside is steeped in Burns. Rabbie, as he is affectionately known, moved with his family from Alloway to several other towns in Ayrshire, including Mount Oliphant, Tarbolton, Irvine, and Mossgiel.

We talked about which one of his over 550 poems I should recite in the competition. "How about 'Tam O'Shanter'?" I suggested. The poem tells the story of Tam, who downed a few too many drams at the local hostelry in Ayr and rode home on his grey mare Meg. Passing the ruins of the Alloway Kirk, he saw witches, goblins, and gremlins coming out of the graves and dancing with the devil. Tam saw a comely spirit and shouted out that he liked her "cutty sark"—short dress. The spirits were incensed and chased Tam, finally catching up with him and his steed as they crossed the old bridge over the River Doon—the Brig o' Doon—and pulled off Meg's tail.

(Some years after I participated in the poetry competition, I took part in the annual Burns ride, in which black-coated equestrians follow the route from the Tam O'Shanter Inn to the old Bridge, pursuing a rider atop a grey mare and attired in period garb with a tammy on his pate. At the end of the ride, the horses graze on the grassy embankment beside the arched stone bridge. Yes, there really is a Brig O'Doon.)

"No," said Mum, "that's too long." She pondered, "There's always the universal favorite from Hogmanay—'For Auld Lang Syne'." The whole world sings Burns to welcome the New Year, starting with the Australians, whose New Year comes first. Her mention of the well-known song brought brought back memories of Hogmanay (New Year's Eve) in Hunter Crescent, when I went first-footing with my parents. The tradition in Scotland is that the "first-foot" over the threshold is tall, dark, and handsome, carrying a bottle of Scotch and a lump of coal—the coal to bring warmth to the neighbor's hearth on the New Year. I tried to reproduce this tradition when I moved to Buffalo, New York, in 1985, by clutching a bottle of Jack Daniels and some charcoal briquettes, but the tradition somehow did not translate.

The Hunter Crescent visits were memorable for hearty greetings and the famous song sung for the sake of old times. Margery and Sid sank quite a few cups o' kindness those nights. It's a good thing we were walking. The Scots, of course, sing all the verses, and when the last verse is sung, "And there's a hand, my trusty fiere! and gie's a hand o' thine!" we cross hands in a circle, joined together to welcome the next twelve months.

I thought of all the wet, spittle-laden, unwelcome cheek kisses from those first-footing jaunts and said, "No, not that one. How about the Haggis poem from Burns suppers?" Across the globe, on or around Burns's birthday, suppers are held to commemorate the great poet. The haggis is piped in with ceremony, and the poem "Ode to a Haggis" recited over the "chieftain o' the puddin' race" lying on a platter. In the third verse the reciter draws a ceremonial knife and plunges it into the steaming dish, saying:

> An' cut ye up wi' ready slight,
> Trenching your gushing entrails bright
> Like onie ditch;
> And then, O what a glorious sight,
> Warm-reekin, rich!

Never having been a fan of haggis, the thought of steaming, pungent entrails turned my stomach.

"I think not."

"I've got it," cried Margery, "'To a Mouse'"—she pronounced it *moose*. "Everyone loves that one."

"To a Mouse, On Turning Her Up in Her Nest With the Plough," was written in 1785 and harkens to Burns's time in farming when he tilled the fields. It is a lovely piece of work, in which Burns bemoans the fact that he has destroyed the poor beastie's house with his ploughshare, and that the mouse will have no material with which to build a new one that winter. He identifies with the rodent as a fellow mortal, but concludes that the mouse is better off as he lives only for the present, whereas Burns remembers the dreary prospects of the past and is fearful of the future.

And so began the coaching. Margery, born close to the Salford docks in the North of England and a purist for pronunciation, took it upon herself to instruct me in Scots dialect. English people often have a lot of trouble with the Scottish *ch* as in *loch*, which they pronounce *lock*. These must be the same people who listen to Johann Sebastian Back, because *Bach* has (almost) the same sound. In phonetics the Scots *ch* is represented by /x/, a voiceless velar fricative. A pedantic phonetician will point out the German *ch* is /ç/.

The Scots *ch* is a sound that begins deep in the lungs, gathers momentum as it passes along the bronchi, and finally exits the vocal cords as if carrying every drop of mucus it picked up along the journey. The way the sound is made has been likened to trying to dislodge a fishbone stuck in the back of the throat.

"Chhhhhhhh," said Margery, sounding like she was gargling, "it's chhhhhhhh."

"Chhkkk," I sputtered, wiping my lips.

"Try again," and once again she emitted the sound, as if she were dredging catarrh from the recesses of her lungs.

I imitated the noise, "Chhhhhhhhhhhhhhhh." Pepe the poodle jerked his head up in surprise, thinking I was in distress.

"Finally!"

Every day I practiced, greeting folk with, "It's a braw, bricht, moonlicht nicht the nicht." They thought I was being congenial when, in fact, I was perfecting my voiceless velar fricative.

The competition day arrived and, as my knees trembled, I described—in the best Scots dialect I could muster—the panic-stricken beastie suddenly made homeless "To thole the winter's sleety dribble/ An' cranreuch cauld." Roughly translated this means To endure the winter's sleet/ And hoar-frost cold.

And when I said "cranreuch," you would have thought I was about to void my rheum into Shylock's beard (we were studying *The Merchant of Venice* in English class) so rumbling and moist was my /x/. I thought I had nailed it.

I returned home after the winners were announced. "Well, how'd you do?" asked Mum.

I bowed my head and shook it, saying:

> But Mousie, thou art no thy lane,
> In proving foresight may be vain:
> The best-laid schemes o' mice an' men
> Gang aft agley,
> An' lea'e us nought but grief an' pain,
> For promis'd joy!

"No joy?"

"That's richt. Nae joy."

"Well, I think you can revert to proper English now, young lady, and say 'No joy.' After all, you weren't dragged up; you were brought up."

Bond...James Bond

I was twelve and my mother fifty-five when we met James Bond. By James Bond, I mean, of course, Sean Connery, the first Bond. It was July of 1970, and Connery was at the height of his fame, having starred as the protagonist secret agent in the first five Bond films. By then he had wooed an assortment of Bond girls, from Honey Ryder in *Dr. No*, to Kissy Suzuki in *You Only Live Twice*. In *Dr. No*, fans were also introduced to 007's friend and ally, Felix Leiter, the CIA agent. During the filming of *Goldfinger*, Sean began his love affair with golf. The script called for Bond playing a round with Auric Goldfinger, while Oddjob caddied. Connery took lessons on a course near Pinewood Studios and became hooked on the game.

The Open Championship in 1970 was held at St. Andrews, birthplace of golf. Connery, a proud Scot, hosted a pro-am at Troon as a lead-up to the Open. Many famous pro golfers travelled to Troon that summer, including Jack Nicklaus, Gary Player, Tony Jacklin, and Lee Trevino. Notable, too, were the amateurs—horror star Christopher Lee and legendary double amputee World War II airman Douglas Bader among them. The pros and the ams graciously gave of their time at the autograph area, set up opposite Troon Ladies' Golf Club, and it was there that I looked up to gaze into the eyes of 6'2" Sean Connery and proffered him my blue autograph book with the pastel-colored pages.

Mother, a member of Troon Ladies', had volunteered to work the event and was assigned the task of marshalling the players to the autograph area at their appointed time. Completing this task she found both irksome and demeaning, for in those days women were not allowed in the front door of the Old Troon clubhouse, so she had to go in the back to find them. "Bloody ridiculous," she would comment when we got home. However, as a primary school teacher, she was an expert in mustering and managed to herd her charges over the course like a sheepdog corralling sheep in the dog trials that took place in the Collins' fields behind our house in Hunter Crescent. I can still imagine her almost nipping their heels.

Maybe she learned that herding skill in one of her first jobs after finishing teacher training, at Briscoe Lane Primary in a suburb of Manchester. For it was there that she helped assemble some of the hundreds of children who were to be evacuated out of the city in 1939 before the bombing began. Manchester was home to heavy industry and a center for commerce—prime target for the blitz that was to come. Part of her task was to make sure her children did not arrive at their new temporary homes in the country with any stowaways on board. "I became an expert in delousing—a champion nit-picker," she later explained to me. She knew the drill, flipping up the hair behind the ears to check for nits (one of lice's favorite warm areas for egg-laying), parting the strands with a fine-toothed comb, and washing lousy pates with anti-parasitic shampoo.

So familiar was I with her mimicry of these actions, that when I arrived in Paris for a French-Ayrshire language summer school in 1972 and the gloved nurse did the same maneuver looking behind my ears, I knew exactly what was up. When I told mother about it after my return home, she was appalled. "You? Lice? Never. How dare they?"

Her knowledge of parasites extended to pinworms, too.

One evening, the year after the pro-am, she arrived home from the shops carrying boxes of many colors of plasticine, a type of modeling clay, a bit like Play-doh but more waxy. You can bend it, create shapes, and manufacture imaginary monsters and the like. She frequently handed it out to her classes for a bit of down time, but, as she pointed out, it had to be replaced on a regular basis.

"Why?" I asked.

"Worms."

"Worms?!"

"Pinworms, to be precise."

She proceeded to explain the life cycle of the pinworm, a diminutive creature about half an inch long that lives in the alimentary tract. The eggs hatch in the small intestine, mature, and migrate to the large intestine, where they reproduce. At night, the females lay their eggs around the anus.

An innocent little ass scratch in the morning, and presto, the eggs are under the finger nails, primed to be passed on to anything touched, whether it be a favorite sweater, bicycle handlebars, or the classroom plasticine. Hence the imperative to change the plasticine on a regular basis, because it was handled so frequently and could be replaced easily.

As Margery wrapped up her explanation of the pinworm lifecycle and the reason to switch out the plasticine, she held me in her gaze and parodied one of Bond's lines from *Diamonds are Forever*, released in 1971. In the movie—the final movie in which Connery played 007—Bond impersonates a diamond smuggler in order to infiltrate the smuggling ring. He arrives in Vegas to pick up the body of his supposed dead brother. Referring to the whereabouts of the stolen diamonds, Leiter asks, "I give up. I know the diamonds are in the body, but where?"

Bond replies, "Alimentary, my dear Leiter."

Margery drew herself to her full height—a good ten inches shorter than Connery—and said "Alimentary, my dear Diane."

Fireballs in my Eucharist

"You'll have to look after the family, you know." My mother's back was turned to me as she made this announcement. I suspended my soup spoon on its way to my mouth, the Campbell's Golden Vegetables steaming in their broth.

"What? Where are you going?" I thought of the fractious argument a few days before that had shuddered the house. Dad had grouted the copper-colored backsplash tiles he had taken days to position *just so* in the bathroom on the landing. Mother wanted a Sun King Bathroom suite—it was the 1970s—and the iridescent copper matched. She always got her way when it came to décor, which explains why her powder room was fitted with an avocado-colored toilet, washbasin, and matching bidet.

Dad descended the stairs, grouting rag in hand, thirsty for water. His rag left a smear on the textured glass half of the door to the kitchen and that mishap sparked it off. Yelling, stomping feet, words to be regretted later, the rag flung across the room into the wall. I retreated to my room till quiet returned to the house.

When I emerged, I saw my dad heading down the hallway to the front door. He was dressed in his camel overcoat, wearing his trilby, and carrying three Chester Barrie suits in his hand, still on hangers.

"Dad, where are you going?" I cried, my throat tight. Mother was still in the kitchen.

"I'm leaving," was all he said. And without a kiss or a hug he was gone. I ran after him down the path, pleading, but he ignored my cries. My shoulders shook with sobs as I trudged back in the house. Mum was still in the kitchen, listening to the play on Radio 4.

"Dad left." She turned, extending a hand to turn off the radio. "He won't be gone long. Just a tiff. He'll get over it." She handed me a tissue

54

and bent a little at the knees to look me in the eyes. "Not to worry, he'll be back."

Three hours passed. She put on her Macintosh and went to look for him. When they both came back half an hour later, neither was speaking. Dad glowered and ascended the stairs heavy-footed. It took days for reconciliation, till their words were not brittle.

So when mother said I would have to look after the family—Dad and the dog—I thought, this is it, they've had the final thunderous fight. I was destined to be the detritus from a broken home. "You're getting divorced?"

"Don't be ridiculous, my love. Your dad and I are very happy. No, I'm going to have surgery." I wasn't sure which part of her statement surprised me more—that they were happy or that she was going to have surgery. She turned her head from the sink to glance at me, her rubber-gloved hands still busy with the dishes. Seeing my chin start to quiver, she added levity (which is probably what saved her marriage). She raised the back of her hand to her forehead, bubbles landing in her hair, and exclaimed in a Cockney accent, "It's them fireballs in me eucharist, love." I stared blankly, an image in my mind of tiny flaming meteors landing in the communion chalice at St. Ninian's—an image that made no sense. "First it's the arthur-itis and now it's the fireballs giving me jip. I have to have a hysterically."

"Fireballs?" I pondered. "Fibroids. I've got it. You have fibroids in your uterus."

"That's what I just told you."

"And you're going to have a hysterectomy." I had deciphered the intentional malapropism.

"Precisely, and your long-suffering father is taking me to Ayr Hospital Sunday to be admitted." She continued, "I'll be gone about a week. You'll be responsible for Dad and Pepe."

Pepe, lying in his bed under the table, thumped his stubby tail on the cushion upon hearing his name. "You'll be in charge of meals. I'll make some ahead of time, put them in the fridge, and then you can heat them up. Easy peasy. You should be able to do that at age thirteen." She regarded me for an instant, "You can cook an egg, can't you?" I nodded my head yes, thinking she should know this. Boiled eggs, scrambled eggs, even poached eggs were in my culinary repertoire. Maybe she was thinking about my pie disaster from Home Economics class. My cheese and potato pie was held up in front of the class by a sadistic teacher as an example of how *not* to garnish. Admittedly, my tomato slices were on the thick side, but I still believe her outrage was out of all proportion to the misdemeanor. This was the same Home Economics teacher who failed me for what I thought was a perfectly acceptable answer to, "How do you make stock?"

"With a Knorr stock cube," was my reply. She thought I was taking the Mickey, but in fact, that's how it was done in our house. When I told Mum about this blot on my copybook, she said. "Well, I'm a working woman. I don't have the time for boiling carcasses and the like."

Dad drove us to the hospital the day before her surgery to be admitted. After she unpacked her small suitcase, she turned to give me a hug. "You know I won't be able to bear you a brother or a sister. You're an only, only child." The melodrama was palpable, a leftover from her amateur dramatic days in Manchester. Dad rolled his eyes; he was used to it.

"Mum, you told me you'd had your tubes tied, and besides, you're fifty-six." I had always wondered about the veracity of the tubal ligation story, considering she had a diaphragm hidden in her top bedside drawer.

"True," she said, "but a little sympathy would be in order." I hugged back and kissed her. Dad did the same, and we left her to change into her hospital gown.

Dad visited every night. On the fourth night he took me along. We found Mum sitting upright, bolstered by pillows and looking a little pale, with a woolen shawl around her shoulders. "Ah, my beloved family," she opened her arms wide in a welcoming embrace, "tell me about your day." We settled in, drawing chairs closer to the bedside. She turned to Sid. "What did you have for lunch? Did you find everything I left for you?"

"I found some mince in the fridge and warmed that up," referring to the hamburger meat on the second shelf.

A frown creased her brow. "Was it in the blue Tupperware or in the porcelain bowl?"

"Tupperware. Why?"

Mother smoothed the sheet beside her. "Em, well, it seems you ate the dog's food."

Dad paled and greened around the gills. He bent at the waist and put his head in his hands, groaning. Considering I was supposed to be in charge of food, I felt compelled to say something. "But Pepe has a fine diet.

His mince is almost as good as ours; only the cut of beef is not quite the same quality." I had seen Mum mincing the beef, hand turning the wheel of the machine clamped to the kitchen table. His meat was just a bit more marbled than ours.

Dad sat up. "It's just the idea of it, eating the dog's dinner."

"I know," murmured Mum, "but I bet Pepe was pleased he had your dinner." They smiled.

"You're right. When are you coming home, pet? I don't want to make that mistake again."

"Tomorrow, I think. That's what the gynecologist said."

And so it was that, fireballs extinguished, Mum came home the next day and sorted out the containers in the fridge. "Next time, if there is a next time, I'll have to label these better." I nodded. She turned to me, "And you will never mention a word of this to anyone—your dad eating the dog food my word. I'm so embarrassed."

"Never."

What Did Your Last Servant Die Of?

She was standing in the doorway to my room, filling the space, legs astride, fists on her hips, her pinny a little damp from washing the dishes, and still wearing her pink Marigold rubber gloves. I knew from that stance that I was in big trouble, mega kaka. Only a few moments before we'd been in the kitchen, and she'd taken a break from washing the dishes to demonstrate the Charleston to me, suds flying everywhere. The mood had changed now.

I was pleasantly occupied putting the finishing touches to my latest model airplane, a Spitfire. Three large display shelves showcased a collection of WW2 model planes, the planes Dad flew in the RAF being my favorites. The tabletop was carefully covered with newspaper, and I had my sable paintbrush poised for the next stroke to the left wing, when the apparition appeared.

"Well, madam, what did your last servant die of?" the apparition said. "When's the last time you cleaned that rabbit's hutch?"

Uh, oh, thought I, she's got a point; I tried a bluff.

"Maybe a couple of days ago."

"And maybe not," she countered. "Get out there right now and change that straw."

I stood up, smoothing the creases in my jodhpurs. I'd ridden at Ayr Stables earlier that day.

That pause was the last straw. "Don't just stand there like a stookie, young lady," likening me to a motionless hay bale. "Move it."

There was no point in arguing. Dissent was futile. I cleaned off my brush with turpentine, packed away my kit, carefully chose a place for the wing to dry, and set off out the back door, down the path to the outbuildings which housed the garden tools and the freezer. Thomas the bunny looked at me quizzically, his jaws at work on his lunch. He used to be named Thomasina, after a cat in one of my favorite Disney movies, but we soon found he had been incorrectly sexed after he started spraying. I gently took him out and let him run around the garden while I mucked out the base of his abode. He enjoyed his spins around the garden, but catching him afterwards was a challenge.

The mucking out and capture completed, I washed my hands and headed back inside the house. Mother greeted me saying, "Well done. Remember doasyouwouldbedoneby. You wouldn't want to live in a dirty house." I recognized the reference to Mrs. Doasyouwouldbedoneby from Charles Kingsley's *The Water Babies*. So—I could make my mother happy, the rabbit happy, and learn the Golden Rule, all in one fell swoop.

They're Knot

I watched the ample rump of the equine in front of me through the constant drizzle of raindrops falling off the brim of my riding hat. The nap of the hat's velvet crown had been flattened by the incessant torrent from above. The bay's haunches moved rhythmically, the hide darkened to a deeper hue by the wetness. My cavernous riding raincoat was no match for the downpour, and I felt my shoulders damp beneath the layers of gabardine and tweed hacking jacket. The suede inner knee patches of my jodhpurs, purposed for extra grip, were now sleek and slippery, with as much extra traction on the saddle as a bar of soap.

Tall pines lined the path well-worn by pony-trekkers, the branches pushed near to the ground by needles laden with rain. The sound of shod hooves on the muddy earth was muffled by the splash of water all around us. When we reached the tarmacadam road bringing us back to the hotel, the rain bounced off its surface and fell to earth again—it rained in stereo. Instead of the scent of pine filling the air, all around was the smell of wet earth, wet clothes, and wet hide.

This was summer in the north of Scotland, specifically the summer of 1970, and I asked myself why we were here. An inner voice answered: To see the ospreys, of course. It was all about birds.

Mother loved animals, all living things, but especially birds. In all our houses, her criterion for the ideal home was that the kitchen sink must be positioned with a view out the window, so she could watch the birds on the feeders. She loved the chaffinches, bluetits, robins, wrens, thrushes, blackbirds, and even pigeons. Mum was fastidious about clearing the ice from the birdbath in winter and keeping it filled. Any leftover dry cereal, or bread butts, were taken out "for the birds." She supplied them with peanuts and suet, admired their babies, and cooed to them lovingly.

One spring afternoon earlier that year we ambled along the Troon promenade. Mum and I had walked down the lane behind Bentinck Drive, past the South Beach hotel, onto the grassy bank, and past the back of the Craiglea Hotel with its resident golden retrievers, which barked their usual greeting, tails waving like plumes. On the beach, our footsteps left a series of small pools as the indentations filled with seawater from the soggy sand. Margery had pointed out the shorebirds paddling in unison along the frothy water's edge, their movements a synchronized scamper. We had seen petite plovers and oystercatchers with their brilliant orange beaks and heard the cawing loud-shrieked gulls, herring gulls, and black-headed gulls.

I saw some little shorebirds foraging at the water's edge. "Sandpipers," I declared.

"They're Knot."

"Not what?"

"Knot."

"NOT WHAT?" I shouted.

"KNOT, K-N-O-T. It's a small shore bird."

"Well, why didn't you say so?"

She sighed, and we sauntered on. She glanced out to sea. "You know, we need to see the ospreys." I knew she was referring to the osprey-viewing center by Loch Garten in Speyside.

"Okey dokey. We've never been, and you've wanted to go for years." I had watched her pore over her RSPB—Royal Society for the Protection of Birds—newsletters featuring the endangered raptors that became extinct in Scotland in the early twentieth century. In 1954 a pair of ospreys settled in Garten from Scandinavia, and the country was gradually repopulated by their offspring.

"Yes," she pulled her head square a little tighter under her chin as the wind caught it. "Let's make it part of the family vacation and plan the route around Boat of Garten."

Dad was informed of the plans when we returned from our constitutional. He was in the living room, his feet propped up on the ottoman, watching the football scores and checking them against his "pools." The pools predated the national lotto, the prizes awarded for the most correct scores. Sid was still clothed in his golfing gear, having battled the wind, the bunkers, and the tenacious broom on Old Troon earlier in the day. His René Lacoste polo shirt was buttoned up to his neck, as was his style.

He glanced up, his pen poised in the air. "Sounds like a good idea. Diane can do some riding, we can sightsee, and we can play golf. It should be fun, providing the weather holds." Ah, the weather. It's always wise to adopt the layered look in Scotland, weather being a fickle beast, easily angered but oh so becoming when tamed.

That summer, Dad steered the car along the northwards route by the west bank of Loch Lomond, fourteen miles longer than heading northeast. Sheets of rain battered the windshield as we neared Luss, one of our favorite resting spots. We honored the British tradition of a picnic in the car. Wispy plumes of steam rose from the hot, milky tea in short cups balanced on the dashboard, creating patterns on the inside of the glass. Outside the windshield, the surface of the loch danced with rain, everything the same dark gray color, the deep water, the mountains, and the sky. Mother poured herself another cup from the thermos, spiked it with a shot of brandy from a flask, and peeled the aluminum foil from her cheese and Branson pickle sandwich. We all watched the sodden scene, jaws masticating. "It's raining," said Dad.

"You think?" I muttered from the back, as I drew patterns with my finger on the passenger window. Mother turned to look at him. "I dread to check the forecast for the rest of the week." Dad nodded, and stared straight ahead. "Better not to even think about it. Bloody waste of money this could turn out to be."

By the shores of Loch Linnhe the downpour had lessened to a drizzle, and as we entered the Cairngorms mountain region, the moisture on the windshield required an occasional swipe from the wiper blades. When we checked in at the hotel, the clouds had at last parted, and rays of sunlight began to dapple the shimmery driveway. "Maybe you could go pony-trekking tomorrow?" said Margery, surveying the list of activities displayed at reception. "I packed your gear."

The first few hours of the trek were idyllic, the scenery through the national forest serene against a backdrop of azure sky dotted with clouds. Had I realized those apparently innocent clouds were cumulonimbus, which portend torrential rain and storms, I wouldn't have been so surprised when the heavens opened with such ferocity.

By the time our sorry trekking party trudged up the gravel driveway to the hotel, my wet clothes had numbed every part of me. An attendant eased me out of the saddle, and Mother met me at the stables carrying a huge bath towel. Its terry cloth felt rough on my face. "Well, kid, let's get you inside and changed." In my room she peeled me out of my riding gear. "Drenched" was her assessment. She grabbed a few clothes hangers from the wardrobe and took my raincoat, jodhpurs, and hacking jacket to hang them up in the bathroom, where, into the night, I would hear the staccato sound of drips splashing into the bathtub.

As I toweled off the rest of me, I heard the rumble of thunder. "Hark, thunder."

"No," she said, "it's just God moving his furniture."

"You borrowed that from Auntie Joan."

"Sure I did. But it's apropos."

"Well, God must be moving an entire town by the sound of it."

She nodded.

The following day the sky had morphed from steel-grey back to blue. Mum peered out of the leaded window of the dining room as she stirred some milk into her porridge. "Today's the day. Ospreys here we come."

Dad looked up from dissecting the bones from his Finnan haddie—green wood and peat-smoked haddock that had been poached in milk. "Well, let's ask for a pack lunch and make a day of it."

At last Mother's wish was gratified. The birds were truly magnificent. A powerful telescope was trained on the four-foot wide nest, high in the branches of a pine tree. An adult bird gyrated its wings to come in for a landing, his feathered legs looking like pantaloons. The almost-bald heads of the chicks were barely visible. Mum was in heaven, silent in her raptor rapture.

Walking trails surrounded the viewing area, so, having had our visual fill of the osprey eyrie, we hiked one of the trails in the Abernethy forest, Dad pushing the tip of the shooting stick into the still-water-laden ground with each step. Mum was on the lookout for other avian species. She knew it was the wrong time of year for the capercaillies, Scotland's largest grouse, but shortly she came to a sudden stop on the path and fumbled with the leather cover for her 15 x 10s. "Crested tits, crested tits," she gesticulated to a tree to her left. Dad came over to her and opened the hinged handle of the shooting stick to reveal a leather seat. While Mum balanced on the narrow saddle, I focused my binos on the spot and shook my head. "Sorry, they're not."

The corners of Mum's mouth twitched into a smile. "Not what?" she said.

We all chuckled, our little family of birders.

When we packed to go home later in the week, as I folded my raincoat, I saw that the dye from the leather covered buckle had left a permanent brown streak from the waist down to the hem, a reminder of the time God moved his furniture around Speyside.

Give the Child Some Laudanum

I'll never know how Mum was able to do it—persuade the white-gloved air stewardess to allow us to fly with the painting on our knees. "Le peinture n'est pas sec," Mum enunciated every syllable in her best accent.

"Ah, mais oui, bien sûr," said the flight attendant, as she nodded, her pillbox hat nodding with her. And so we flew the distance from Paris Orly to Glasgow Abbotsinch with the framed still-damp canvas horizontal on our laps. The plane was an Air France Caravelle—an awesome craft because the rear passenger stairs descended from the center of the fuselage under the tail, and I was bound and determined to exit by the back stairs just for the experience.

Mum and I were returning from our Easter 1971 trip to Paris—one of the jaunts we took without Sidney because he had too much tailoring work to do. For weeks beforehand, Mum had cloistered herself in the front room with her Berlitz lessons, and it was paying off now. Clearly, the crisply dressed stewardess understood that putting the oil in the overhead bin would smudge the paint.

We'd had a full week in the capital on our organized tour. From the options in the glossy color catalog, Mum had chosen a quaint hotel on a cobbled street in Montmartre. Every morning, our breakfast, comprised of pastries, with café au lait for Mum and hot chocolate for me, was brought to our small room with the slanted ceiling. Hot crumbly croissants left slivers of butteriness on our lips. Wonderful. When we left the hotel to explore the city, we passed leather-clad women exposing lots of thigh covered in fishnet hose, my introduction to ladies of the night.

As we flew home, I thought back on our magical week. We had ambled along the Champs Elysees, hearing the strains of the Joe Dassin recording about that avenue coming from inside one of its restaurants; had sat at sidewalk cafes eating sandwiches aux jambon; and I had marveled as Mother added water to her Ricard, turning it from clear to milky opaque.

But it was our visit on that last day to the Place du Tertre filled with street artists that was the most memorable experience of the week. A brightly-colored painting caught Mum's eye: the brushstrokes depicted the dome of the Basilica of Sacré-Coeur bathed in light in the background, while in the foreground, a smartly dressed lady in a peach-colored suit and high heels walking her poodle across the square towards the café table with the striped umbrella. It must have reminded her of our poodle Pepe, for the deal was done in minutes, and hours later we were in the Caravelle with the street scene on our knees.

My pleasant thoughts were intruded upon, though, by a terrible migraine headache that intensified throughout the flight because of the screaming infant behind us. The descent only made the screams worse. Mother grew irritable, starting to sniff, a sure sign of her impatience. Finally, she turned round and said to the hapless mother, "Give that child some laudanum."

"I doubt she's got any Tincture of Opium on her," I said trying to placate Mother. "Besides, I'm sure it's his ears with the altitude. Infants' Eustachian tubes don't always work well."

Mum settled down, remembering my own ear problems and need for grommets as a young child. She looked down at her painting and smiled, her enjoyment of the art assuaging her annoyance at the wails behind her. "I'm sure those are ears he'll grow into," she concluded.

An Irish Mess

We were off on another summer holiday, this time to Ireland, only fourteen miles from the tip of the Mull of Kintyre to the coast of Northern Ireland as the crow flies. Getting there, nonetheless, involved a ferry, since we were taking our car. Mum always loved ferries: listening for the sounds of the waves hitting the hull, feeling the wind messing her hair, and sniffing the tangy, salty air. She enjoyed being on the water. We drove to Stranraer, a port further south along the Ayrshire coast, where we took the ferry to Larne, at the time there being no terminal in Troon, making our travelling distance certainly over fourteen miles, since we were not crows.

Mother had chosen the itinerary, a leisurely drive through Irish countryside, with Dad doing all the driving as usual. Larne to Belfast, on to Newry, then over the border into the South, on to Dublin, then Waterford, Cork, Tipperary, Limerick, and then back to the North. Mum and Dad planned some activities along the way to satisfy my thirteen-year-old's fanaticism for horses: a stay at a Connemara horse farm, pony treks, and a ride on a buggy pulled by a grand steed. They had arranged some golf, too, to keep us all happy.

We'd been merrily engaged in a sing-a-long to "It's a Long Way to Tipperary," when I noticed the car was wheezing up the hill. For the past several miles strange grunting noises had been coming from under the bonnet—a Walter Mitty-esque pocketa-pocketa sound. Dad's brows creased in consternation. "I think we're missing a cylinder," he said.

Not having a clue what he was talking about, I chimed in from the back seat, "Well, wouldn't we have heard it fall out?"

"No, you daft Mickey," said Mum, gripping the hand rest above the door more tightly. "He means all the cylinders are not firing." With that diagnosis, the car shuddered to a halt, steam hissing from the engine, and we had an instant traffic jam on the narrow road ascending the hillside.

"Bloody hell!" exclaimed Dad. He glared at Mum, as if she were responsible. "Don't look at me with that tone of voice," she countered. "It's not my fault." Chastised, Dad leapt out to open the bonnet, plumes of steam engulfing him.

"Oh, God, Sidney," Mum was out of the car with him now. "This is a Mess with a capital M." She waved ineffectually at the clouds coming from the engine.

"We better call the AA." Dad was referring to the Automobile Association. "I have to get to a phone."

In the meantime, the cars behind us managed to creep by our disabled Rover on the narrow road. Dad flagged one down and asked for a lift to the nearest town. Seeing our predicament, no reasonable person could refuse.

It was probably an hour before he returned, riding with the recovery and towing vehicle. Mum and I had been playing I Spy in the back of the car, though we were running out of subjects: hill, grass, trees, tires, windshield, etc.

The mechanic parked in front of us and inspected the engine. "Hmm, looks like you've blown the head gasket." Dad looked crestfallen. "That'll be a pretty penny," he euphemized, knowing it was really going to be quite ugly.

"Well, it has to be done." Mother was always practical.

And with that, we boarded our rescuer's truck and watched as he readied his gear for towing. I don't remember what the nearest town was, but whether it was Tipperary or not, it was a long way.

The Open Championship

There were hushed tones in the Clubhouse Bar that late afternoon as the final pair reached the eighteenth green. The day had started out rainy, with a myriad of multi-colored golf umbrellas protecting the spectators and the caddies vainly attempting to shield their pros from the raindrops. It was a day full of expectancy and suspense. Tom Weiskopf had led each of the preceding three days of the 1973 Open Championship, the 102nd. If he finished with a total score of 275, 13 under par, he would beat the lowest Open score ever, set by Arnold Palmer the last time the Open was played at Troon, in 1962.

My parents and I were gathered around a table watching the action on the eighteenth green, whispering, lest our voices could somehow reach the players through the glass. "Gently Bentley," Mother purred to a player as he made his putting stroke. "Oh, oh. Too fast," she said as the ball rolled a foot past the hole. Thanks to my dad's membership, we sat in the plush interior of the clubhouse of Old Troon Golf Club. He'd been on the waiting list for membership a long time, but now that he was in, he played as often as his work would allow. In 1973 the Club had not yet been awarded royal status. That was granted in 1978, the centenary of the club, which was thereafter known as Royal Troon. Dad often treated us to lunch at the club, starting in the Ailsa Room with its comfy easy chairs and vast windows overlooking the course and the adjacent Marine Hotel, before going through to the wood-paneled dining room, at one end of which hung a portrait of Dr. Highet, the first Honorary Club Secretary.

Mum and I were members of the Ladies' Golf Club Troon, founded in 1882. The Ladies' Clubhouse, on Crosbie Road, overlooks the seventeenth fairway of Royal Troon in one direction and Portland Course in the other. As a family, we mostly played Portland together. Sometimes in the summer we'd go out for nine holes in the long evenings. If the dog joined us, we'd play the nine-hole "children's course." Pepe was a willing participant till he was hit once by an errant drive of Mum's. The bathrooms of the Ladies' Clubhouse included a quaint porcelain foot bath, about three feet by three feet, where players could cleanse their weary feet after a long round. The dining room, to the upstairs front of the clubhouse, provides welcome respite and a much-needed cup of tea, served in china sporting the Ladies' Club motto and crest.

The Open Championship was exciting from the start. On the first day the veteran golfer Gene Sarazen holed-in-one at number eight, the Postage Stamp, so-called for its small putting surface. Johnny Miller was lying second after three days and was a favorite as he'd won the US Open at Oakmont in Pennsylvania the month before. Always a contender, Jack Nicklaus, who had won the Open twice on Scottish soil, had birdied four of the first seven holes on the last day. He had finished with a round of 66 the previous year at Muirfield, so a Nicklaus "charge" was certainly possible.

We could see from the leader board what was going on around the course. Weiskopf sank a birdie putt at number six "Turnberry," a 577-yard par 5, to take him to 12 under par, three strokes ahead of Miller. The Ryder cup veteran British player Neil Cole was having a great day, and the American Bert Yancey was lying 8 under after seven holes. Another birdie for Weiskopf at the eleventh hole took him to 13 under, three strokes ahead of his nearest challenger with seven holes to play. He would not remain at 13 under for long. A bogey at number thirteen, "Burmah," a 468-yard par 4, brought him back to 12 under. Miller also dropped a shot at number fifteen, taking him to 9 under. The rain had stopped by then, giving the players some relief.

From our comfortable vantage point within the clubhouse, we had watched the great Nicklaus birdie on the eighteenth, much to the thrill of the gallery, who roared. He entered the clubhouse at 8 under with a final score of 280. The crowd erupted again when Coles putted out to end 9 under. By then the rain had started up again.

Weiskopf maintained his three-stroke lead through the seventeenth hole, almost certain to be the victor, especially when Miller's second shot found the bunker to the right of the eighteenth green. After Weiskopf hit his second shot onto the green, the crowd started to buzz. As he and Miller walked up the eighteenth fairway, the rain was heavy, and Tom's caddy held a green and white striped umbrella over him, contrasting colors to Weiskopf's black and yellow. Applause and cheers surrounded the smiling leader as he gave thumbs up to the spectators and clapped his trusty caddie on the shoulder. We were cheering inside, too, caught up in the historic moment. Miller hit a beautiful bunker shot to within two feet of the hole. Weiskopf's long putt from the edge of the green ended up a similar distance from the hole. He marked his ball, as tradition dictates that the leader putts out last.

Miller, clad in blue check pants, grey sweater, and red tartan tammy, holed his par putt easily and doffed his cap to the cheering crowd. Mum leaned into me, saying, "In two shakes of a lamb's tail this will be over." Holding our breath, we watched Weiskopf's smooth putt. It made the four-inch drop, and the Open was over. The gallery was on its feet, the applause rattling the windows. Palmer's record was equaled. There was a new Open Champion. As Harry Carpenter said in his BBC commentary, "The old Guard had better watch out." But the old guard was doing fairly well that day, too. Arnie, at age forty-three played a round of 72 on the last day, par for the course.

In 2004, I was in Troon for the 133rd Open, this time walking the course. For the 145th Open, in 2016, I watched part of the last day of play from within Royal Troon Clubhouse, and I cast my mind back to that day forty-three years earlier when we attended as a family. As I saw the players putt on 18, I said to myself, "Gently Bentley, not too fast."

The Mother Formerly Known as Margery

I timetabled my homework around what was on TV. Mum knew this; in fact, I'd learned it from her. Weekly, she would buy the *Radio Times*, which detailed the shows on BBC and ITV. For years there were only four TV stations in the UK—BBC1, BBC2, ITV1, and ITV2, so what was on the box was to be savored. Margery would pore over the pages of the magazine, circling with a Biro the shows she intended to watch that week and planning her evenings accordingly.

Sitcoms and variety shows were her favorites—*The Liver Birds, To the Manor Born, The Two Ronnies, Steptoe and Son, Frankie Howerd, The Morecombe and Wise Show*, and *The Good Life*.

As for me, I enjoyed the comedies and music shows, above all, *Top of the Pops. TOTP* came on every Thursday night. Hosted by Jimmy Saville, at that time a beloved celebrity (no one knew about the sex scandals until decades later), the show featured the current hits, with bands performing live on stage.

One Thursday evening in 1973, I wandered into the living room to catch the show, which came on at 7 p.m. Dad reclined on the couch and Mum sat in one of ash-backed Ercol chairs, chewing on a Cadbury's Turkish Delight . She glanced up as I came in. "Don't you have homework?"

Well, of course, I had homework, but I figured out I could spare thirty minutes to get up to date with the hit parade. She followed her question with a gesture I knew well. Her left hand circled in a horizontal plane while her right hand pinched her nose. After a few revolutions, the left hand motion ceased, and her right hand reached above her head to pull the chain on an imaginary high cistern. This was the Margery sign for,

"If you don't do your homework, you will end up cleaning toilets." I had seen it a hundred times if I'd seen it once. It was a gesture unique to her, as far as I knew.

Churchill had his V for Victory; Carol Burnett tugged her ear to say thanks and I love you to her grandmother, and Margery Radford had the high toilet flush. It was a symbol of failure to her, of lack of perseverance. The artist formerly known as Prince came to be identified by his peculiar love symbol for a few short years in the 1990s.

This is not to say that Mum had any bias against janitorial services. Everyone needs them; our living and work spaces have to be clean. She just had greater aspirations for her first and only born. I was destined to be the first of my immediate family to go to university. Mum had been educated at teacher training college in Leeds, and Dad left school at fourteen to be an apprentice tailor in Manchester.

Of course, my mother did raise me to respect people who worked in all manner of jobs, including janitorial services and so-called low skilled labor. In 1994, while I was on faculty at Washington University in St. Louis, I had dropped into the cafeteria for a spot of lunch. In front of me at the cash register was another physician, so inflated with his own importance he filled the narrow space between the checkouts. He was having a hissy fit, and for whatever reason, decided to take out his bad day on the cashier.

"Can't you ring this up faster? Don't you realize doctors are essential to running this hospital?" His face reddened just as the cashier's grew pale. Both were wide-eyed.

I tapped him on the shoulder. "Don't you realize this hospital can't run without housekeeping? Everyone contributes." He sneered silently at me, grabbed his tray, and scuttled off. The x-ray technician in line behind me slapped me on the back.

"Way to go!"

The cashier comp'ed my cup of tea and pressed the change into my palm with a hand hug.

I negotiated my position regarding homework with my mother. "I have an hour left for my essay on the poetry of WWI. I can get that done between *Top of the Pops* and the *Nine O'clock News* and still have time for a few trig problems." My rationale struck me as argument-proof.

She took another bite of her gelatinous purple chocolate-covered confection and contemplated my answer. "All right, my little cauliflower, half an hour of Gary Glitter, TRex and 10cc, and then back at it."

We'd made a deal. Negotiation complete.

A Pause for Silent Prayer

St. Ninian's Episcopal Church in Troon stands solidly on the west side of Bentinck Drive, its red Mauchline sandstone walls a buttress against the winds that whip down the boulevard, bending the trees on Bentinck Crescent to a forty-five degree angle. These thick walls framed my christening, confirmation, and early years of worship. On passing through the arched heavy oak front door, on the inner side of which is carved a mouse—the signature of the carver, Mouse Thompson—the worshipper enters the sacred sanctuary.

In my earliest memories of services there, I sat in the wicker children's chairs after we shuffled in from Sunday school, to an all-too-prominent position in the front of the nave. Once older, I sat further back in the adult version of the children's chairs, also wicker-seated but joined in the back to form a kind of pew, and knelt for prayer on the embroidered individual kneelers. It was from one of these kneelers on one occasion that I keeled over into the red-carpeted aisle in a dead faint, suspending the service. It was into that same aisle that Margery leapt, sprinted to the back of the church, then high-tailed it out down the path to our house 150 yards away because, I learned later, she had a chicken "roasting" in the cooker but had forgotten to turn the oven on.

Margery and Sidney chose St. Ninian's because they both worshipped in the Church of England when they lived south of the border, and the Episcopal Church is the Anglican Church up north. Mum would ask sometimes at parties, "What's an Ecopalian?" The bemused listener would shake his head, indicating he didn't know, at which time she would explain, "It's an Episcopalian with the piss knocked out of him." Uproarious laughter would erupt. Typically, she'd had a tipple when she said this.

Sidney and Margery were often hosts for the after-church-at-St.-Ninian's-but-before-Sunday-lunch-cocktail-party. The party preparation would start early Sunday morning. "Come and help me make some hors d'oeuvres," she'd shout from the kitchen. But she pronounced it *horses doovers*, even though she knew perfectly well how to say it properly—all those hours she'd spent with her Berlitz tapes. She had her tools arrayed—toothpicks, cheese cubes, Ritz crackers, and the like. "I have sausage rolls in the oven," she announced. "Help me make these sausage-cheese bites." Before we began, she placed her hands on her hips and sighed, saying, "A pause for silent prayer." We both took a few deep breaths before the culinary creation started.

I mimicked what she was doing—spearing first a diminutive chipolata sausage, then a cube of sharp cheddar on the end, transferring it to the platter covered with a white paper doily. There were tart gherkins, too, and olives stuffed with pimentos. On another tray were cubes of milky, crumbly Cheshire cheese with a topknot of pickled cocktail onion. The sausage rolls were on a timer so they would be ready when the church service ended.

While we were busy in the kitchen, Dad would prepare a makeshift bar on a hostess trolley in the lounge—the grand room to the front of the house, with the Greek key cornice and the teak gramophone in the corner. From there he would pour stiff G and Ts, gin and Angostura bitters, whisky and water, the occasional lager shandy, and even a martini. He polished the crystal with a linen dish towel, holding each glass up to the light streaming through the bay windows. My job was to circulate among the guests at these events—proffering the hors d'oeuvres trays, gathering empty glasses to be refilled with another libation, and generally just keeping things moving along. This left my parents free for scintillating conversation, merriment, and catching up on the local gossip. I was also responsible for clearing up afterwards, and vacuuming the carpet—a child's work is never done.

Although she sometimes made fun of her religion, Mother loved St. Ninian's. She served in many roles there: worshipper, part-time Sunday school teacher, at-a-pinch pianist, fundraiser at the tombola, donor, and supplier of baked goods. Dad, on the other hand, could be crusty about church. "It's all about an argument with the vestry," he'd say, never giving me the full details. Apparently, even long after the members of the vestry had turned over a few times, he never felt good about attending, which I thought was sad, since my mother then often had to attend solo.

Through the years my parents saw several rectors come and go. The first, Jimmy McGill, arrived in Troon just in time to christen me at the marble font in the back of the church, under the stained glass window donated by the Walkers (of Johnny Walker Scotch). Around the base of the font is carved the dedication by the donor James Harling Turner in memory of his parents, sister and brother, and the quote from Matthew 19:14: "Suffer little children to come unto me and forbid them not for of such is the kingdom of heaven."

Visiting the church with my partner Pam in 2011, I saw the same small chairs, the same conjoined pews, and the same stone font. The sunlight streamed through the leaded glass windows, illuminating some of the plaques commemorating those lost in the Great War. In the church hall we found the stone donated by Mrs. Townsend, who lost both sons, their sacrifice in 1917 twenty-two days apart. It was a somber moment as we contemplated her grief. Had Margery been with us, she would have said, "A pause for silent prayer."

I wonder if she always stopped to pray, or sometimes just to rest. Especially on our walks later in her life, she stopped frequently, having trouble with impaired circulation to her legs that was the result of years of smoking even though she had quit decades earlier. Her days of sprinting down the aisle were over by then. But whenever she said, "A pause for silent prayer," I usually prayed, thankful to be able to hear the gulls overhead and the rush of the waves on the beach. After a moment, we'd resume our perambulation along the promenade, linked arm in arm.

Dodds Coach Trip

"We're taking the bus. I've decided." Mother's pronouncement filled the room and grabbed our attention. Now Margery was not, in general, a bus-taker, preferring to be chauffeured by Sid, although during those drives she would shield her eyes, or even close them ("I'm resting my eyes"), and her left hand would be white-knuckled as she gripped the hand rest above the passenger door.

We had planned a trip to the Edinburgh Military Tattoo, an annual festival of music and pageantry held on the esplanade of the centuries-old Edinburgh Castle. She continued, "Do you remember the last time we tried to park in Edinburgh?" Sadly, I did. We'd gone for a day of shopping on Princes Street, the grand boulevard with the backdrop of the castle on top of the hill, across the road from the shops. But before we could embark on retail therapy, we had to park. Parking spots were few and far between even on an ordinary day, and when she saw one near Charlotte Square, Mother commanded Sid to stop the car so she could leap out and claim the spot while he maneuvered the motorcar. Needless to say, there were quite a few other drivers, whom I could see from my vantage point in the back seat, who felt the spot was theirs, not ours. They shook their fists and made other gestures in her direction. Margery completely ignored them and motioned Sid to reverse into the spot, as I tried to slide below view of the irate drivers.

"You have a point, my dear," conceded Dad. I'm sure her question had evoked in him the same mental image. She continued, "Well, I'm up to high doh with parking, so we're going on the Dodds coach. Put that in your pipe and smoke it." We looked at her, surprised that she was so emphatic, since neither Dad nor I had voiced an objection. "Furthermore,

I'm putting my foot down with a heavy hand on this one!" She sat down, a little breathless.

"Yes, my love," said Dad, "that will be just fine." Discussion over.

The Dodds family of Troon had been in the transport business since 1910, so they knew how to do this. To this day they have excursions to the Tattoo, which takes place every August as a part of the Edinburgh International Festival. The Festival gathers performing artists from all over the world, stunning audiences with dance, opera, music, and theater. Along with dozens of other passengers, we boarded the green and pale yellow coach at Dodds depot on Portland Street. The coach was plush, with Dodds logo-ed head rest covers and expansive skylights. It was a smooth ride, and after we disembarked on Johnston Terrace, it was a relatively short walk to Castlehill on the Royal Mile and the entrance to the Castle. A crowd of visitors from all over the globe thronged around us.

Tattoo, by the way, does not refer to body ink. It relates to the Dutch term "tap-toe," toe being pronounced "too," meaning, "last orders," or "close the beer tap." The British Army encountered the term "tap-toe" when they were stationed in Flanders in the 1700s and adopted the practice of sounding a signal (played by the drum corps or pipes and drums) to local hostelry owners to cut off the beer flow so their soldiers could get a good night's sleep. Over the years, the term morphed into "tattoo," meaning a military performance of music.

As we ascended Castlehill, I looked up at the huge grandstands surrounding the esplanade on three sides. Temporary, at that time they had a capacity of over eight and a half thousand and took two months to erect. New similar-capacity steel-framed stands have been used from 2011 onwards, their manufacture reducing assembly and dismantling time from two months to one. The show lasts ninety minutes—an hour and a half of music, dancing, and, of course, the skirl of the bagpipes. Some shows have featured fiddlers, Chinese dragons, the Top Secret Swiss Army Band, Zulu warriors, Maori dancers, motorcycle displays, the Citadel Band, the US Marines, and steel drums. That year we were treated to a dancing display by the Regiment of Gurkhas, who showed their skill controlling their traditional weapon, the khukuri.

There can be no sight more thrilling, however, than the massed pipes and drums of the invited bands and regiments marching out of the Castle archway, flanked by the statues of the great Scottish heroes Robert the Bruce and William Wallace and huge flaming torches, fanning out to fill the esplanade as the air throbs with sound. The 2005 Tattoo featured thirteen bands, one of the largest gatherings of pipes and drums in the history of the event, which dates to 1950. Bands of all six regular infantry divisions of the Scottish Division of the British Army were present. In some shows, participation of the British Armed Forces in conflicts overseas is honored, such as the commemoration of the Battle of Trafalgar, the Falklands War, or the Middle East.

After the close of the show, we wended our way slowly back the way we came, small flotsam in a sea of people. We had sung "God Save the Queen" and "Auld Land Syne," watched the lowering of the flag, heard the bugle call, seen the lone piper high on the Half Moon Battery piping a lament, and applauded as the non-playing performers marched down the Esplanade to the tune of "Scotland the Brave." The massed military bands had marched off to the traditional Scottish farewell song, "No Awa' Tae Bide Awa,'" and, finally, the massed pipes and drums, in all their magnificent glory, spats still crisp, with kilts flaring, had marched off to the tune of "The Black Bear." We were, all three of us, exhausted by the climb, the crowds, but also the patriotic thrill of it all.

Reaching the coach, Mum wearily mounted the stairs, saying to our driver, "Home James, and don't spare the horses."

"Aye, Mrs. Radford, " he replied.

The Things You See When You Don't Have Your Gun

Dad pressed the accelerator down to the floor to push past the lorry, which splashed waves of water onto the Rover as we sped northeast up the A77 to Glasgow. It was a dismal, dreich day, the wipers barely able to keep up with the torrent on the windshield. Mother held her hands up in front of her eyes, a position she often assumed when Dad drove. As visibility decreased, his speed incrementally increased. "Have we passed it?" She referred to the lorry, speaking through her hands.

"Yes, we're clear," said Dad, eyes fixed on the road.

I sat in the back seat, observing the rain-soaked brown and white Ayrshire cows grazing in the fields alongside us. Their jaws masticated in the sideways movement of ruminants.

It was 1974. We were on our way to the University for my medical school entrance interview. The national university entrance matching program, Universities Central Council on Admissions (UCCA), had matched me with my first choice—Glasgow. At age sixteen, however, I'd be one of the youngest in the class. An interview was required. I guess they wanted to see what they were getting. That morning I dressed carefully— Liberty of London floral print blouse; grey A-line skirt tailored by Sidney Radford, Tailor and Cutter; 15 dernier hose; matching pumps (or court shoes as Mum called them, not that she'd ever been to Court); and my best Jaeger camel-colored coat. I thought I looked great.

To complete the outfit I'd "borrowed" some hairspray I found in Mum's powder room, spraying clouds liberally around my locks.

Dad slowed down from faster to fast as the rain eased off. Mum's shoulders relaxed, and she let her hands drop. She took her eyes off the road (although still aware of lorries alongside), brought down the vanity mirror to check her lipstick, and surveyed my reflection. She looked back at herself, then back at me. I smiled in response. She snapped the mirror and sun visor back into place and sniffed. Ominous. Her sniffs usually indicated disapproval. I fidgeted, suddenly intrigued by the nap of my coat, smoothing it this way and that.

A few moments passed as we crossed the barren, rolling landscape of the Fenwick moor. The dairy cows had been replaced by Blackface sheep, heads down nibbling what grass there was. She brought the mirror down again, and this time held me in her gaze. I could stand it no longer. "What?" I asked. "What's wrong?" I felt self-conscious and conspicuous.

"It's your hair, my little Brussels sprout. What *did* you do to your hair?"

"Oh, do you like it?" I was hopeful. "I found some hairspray in your powder room." Mum's powder room was en-suite to the master bedroom. It contained a washbasin, WC, and a bookcase with reading material I wasn't supposed to find, like *Everything You Wanted to Know About Sex But Were Afraid to Ask* and *Valley of the Dolls*. Of course, those books were well-thumbed, in part by me, as I sought all the best bits. I wonder if she ever noticed.

"I don't have any hairspray in the powder room."

"Yes, you do. It was in a golden color aerosol by Elizabeth Schwarzkopf, in a small container." I saw her shoulders stiffen. She sniffed. "Ah," she said, "That's not hairspray. That's to put an extra sheen on your hair and must be used sparingly." She turned in her seat and held index and thumb up close together. "Sparingly. How much did you use?" I thought back to the beautification process.

"Not sparingly."

By now, Dad had adjusted his rearview mirror to get a look at the apparition in the back seat. I saw his eyes widen. He swallowed, then coughed. His face was stony. "Oh my God," he said. I could stand it no longer.

Gathering courage, I inched over to see myself in the mirror. "Oh, oh." What looked back at me appeared to be the image of someone who had not washed her hair for a week. The cheeks of my reflection turned red. My hair had no sheen; it was lank and drab. My heart pounded in my chest.

"Now what?"

The tower of Bute Hall appeared on the horizon, and the sun peeked out now the rain had stopped. A rainbow curved over Gilmorehill, a halo around the University.

"Maybe that's a good sign." Dad pointed to the rainbow trying to cheer me up. My stomach felt like it had fallen on the pavement and been trampled by shoppers on Sauchiehall Street.

"I'll never get in now. I'm done for. They'll think I don't wash. My career is over."

"Don't go overboard," said Mum. "You don't even have a career yet."

She did have a point.

Dad parallel parked into a space on University Avenue. They both turned round to face me. "I'll rearrange your hair so it looks like it's part of the style," she said as she got into the back seat with me and sculpted with her Mason Pearson brush, all the while pursing her lips. At last she seemed satisfied. "If we only had a beret. But we don't, so that's that."

They walked with me across the quadrangle and through the echoing cloisters to the interview room. A hug for each of them and I turned, saying, "I'm going in."

Dad grinned. "Be like the RAF, pet: Fly in, do what you have to do, and get the hell out." I parodied a salute.

An hour later I rejoined them at the car. "I'm exhausted; let's go home."

It was about fifteen minutes into the silent journey that Mum eventually asked, with arched eyebrows, "Well?"

"Hard to say, really. They said they'd send a letter."

"You know we'll all laugh about this in times to come," Margery continued. "I'm sure you'll get in, not to worry. But the hair thing: Serves you right for going into my powder room in the first place, madam." She looked at me again in the vanity mirror and shook her head, her lips smiling. "The things you see when you don't have your gun."

Gin a Body, Meet a Body.

There's a section of the A77, on the drive southwest to Troon from Glasgow, where you first glimpse the horizon, the interface between the sea and the sky. The view can be spied on the journey at around Hansel Village, a home for children with learning disabilities, which has stood on the left hand side of the highway since 1963. That expanse of water always takes my breath away, and my heartbeat quickens when I see it. It's a wide bay, from Mull of Kintyre to the north to the Heads of Ayr to the south. The massif of the mountain range on the Isle of Arran pushes up towards the heavens, and rising darkly out of the shimmering sea is the inverted bowl-shaped island Ailsa Craig, like a Christmas pudding in the ocean.

Such was the view that greeted me that Saturday morning in 1974 during my first term of medical school as I drove home. As I sped along the highway, I soaked in the sight, even as my eyes stung from the stench of the dead body in the back seat. Glancing in the rearview mirror, I saw the lifeless eyes staring back at me, the chin bearing a straggly beard. It was a supremely ugly face. I knew I was in for "what for" when I got home with the corpse; it was a mistake to bring it home.

I pressed my foot on the accelerator, urging the Sunbeam Sport to a speed it was barely capable of. When I pulled up in front of the house, I thought I might as well carry the body in, get it over with. Face the music. I opened the car door and grabbed the cardboard box, the partially dissected catfish half-wrapped in pages of the *Glasgow Herald*.

Scurrying up the concrete path to the glass front door, I could see my mother approaching down the hallway from the kitchen, wiping her hands on her apron. "Darling, how was your journey?" she asked as she opened the door. Before I could answer, her eyes glanced down at my burden, and as I rushed past her to get to the back of the house and the outbuildings, she caught a whiff of formalin.

"What the h........what a smell!" She pointed to the back door. "Out, out with it. Out damned spot," she quoted Shakespeare, her hands flapping at the air in front of her, in an effort to move its pungency around. "Obnoxious effluvium! Get that thing out of the house."

Dad, hearing the commotion, got up from his position in front of the TV in the family room and came into the hallway, too. "Good grief! What in God's name is that?"

I stopped to tell him about our Cranial Nerves of the Catfish class and was about to show him what I had dissected thus far, when Mother cried from behind me, "Don't stop her; she can tell you later. She's on her way to the outbuildings with that, that...thing." She gyrated her arms, propelling me forward.

The outbuildings, sand-colored brick, were to the right of the garden path leading to the detached garage. At some point in the house's history in the early twentieth century, they probably held garden tools, a workbench, and the like. One had a large sink for laundry, the other the chest deep freeze. I laid the dark gray Clyde catfish in the sink for further dissection later that day, thinking that one dead fish was causing a whole lot of trouble.

When I came back in the house, Mum had the kettle on for tea and had calmed down, somewhat. "Whatever possessed you, oh Miss Clever Clogs, to bring a dead catfish home? You stunk the house out."

I explained that it was a complicated dissection and, in order to finesse the last few tendrils of nerves, I had no choice but to bring my homework down to the coast. "It was either that or not come home this weekend."

"I see. You were between Scylla and Charybdis."

I nodded, knowing that a lesser person would have said, *between a rock and a hard place.* "Clearly, and I chose Scylla, the sea monster. Well, river monster to be exact, with very long barbels."

She shrugged. "Well, I'm glad you came home, but get that damn Scylla finished this afternoon, dispose of it, and then we can enjoy the rest of the weekend."

Dad joined me in the shed for a short while as I unwrapped my dissecting kit from its sage green cloth roll-up container: forceps, sharp-tipped scissors, a probe to explore foramina, scalpels. I selected my tools carefully and set to work, freeing the fibrous tissue around the axons to expose the length of the nerves. Long after Dad had left me to myself, I sketched the final result into my workbook and called it a day. The western sky was tinged with amber as I walked back up the path to the house.

On entering I heard the TV droning the football scores, catching a few words here and there—Queen of the South, Rangers, Celtic, Hibernian, Hearts, the reporter read off the results in a monotone. Dad had fallen asleep in front of the box and only the dog received the scores. From the kitchen came the theme for the radio show *The Archers* as Mum prepared the dinner. I crept into the kitchen and hugged her from behind as she stood at the counter chopping carrots. "What's for dinner?"

"Well, you can bet your life it's not fish, madam." She turned and smiled. "Chicken à la king."

And as the dusk turned to night, we gathered around the dining table off the kitchen. The remainder of my weekend at home was uneventful in comparison to my arrival; trips into town, walks along the promenade, a few holes of golf with Dad. On Sunday evening I steered the Sunbeam back onto the A77, heading northeast. In the rear view mirror I saw the reflection of the bay I loved.

Margery would have a story to tell that week at Malcolm Campbells when she bought her apples. "You won't believe what Diane bought home from medical school at the weekend." I imagined her pausing for effect. "A body."

Part Three

Wilson Avenue

Satisfying her wanderlust, when I was in my late teens, Mother decided to move two miles back to the same part of town as Hunter Crescent. This home was another bungalow, but with pebble-dash covering the brick. I was living in Glasgow completing medical school and internship by this time, so this was never my home in the same way that our others in Troon were. Still, I remember for my graduation that Auntie Joan came to visit, and the soft tinkle of the ice cubes in her gin and tonic as she reclined in the plush, upholstered easy chair in the living room. It was also in this home that we celebrated my twenty-first birthday, complete with a personalized "This Is Your Life" scrapbook and cassette tape compiled by my friend Barbara, based on the popular TV show.

When I came home for the weekends, I brought my cat Sylvester, who enjoyed the back garden and the floral-print swing seat. The location of the house provided easy access to the Fullarton House grounds for walks. Mum and Dad's friends, Sir Thomas and Lady Symington, were not far away on Lady Margaret Drive.

Mother's cousin Kathy Conboye would often visit, and my mind's eye still bears the image of them strolling down the sidewalk, on their way to Fullarton Woods, the street lined by cherry trees with their fluttery blossom.

The Skelington

Mum plopped down in one of the Parker Knoll chairs in the living room, brought her pale green ceramic teacup up to her lips, her other hand suspending the saucer beneath, and said, "All right then, tell me all about it." There are some events better recounted to mothers in person than over the phone. Every daughter knows this. Information conveyed in aliquots can assuage worry. This was one story I knew had to be told in person.

I'd driven down to Troon from Glasgow that Friday night. There had been a freeze Thursday night and, as always, the locks of my Sunbeam Sport froze. On mornings like these there was only one entry that I could pry open, the hatchback window. I wiggled through, no doubt looking like I was diving into the metallic lavender-hued car. Turning myself upright in the back seat, I squeezed into the driver's seat and set off southwest. In my mind's eye I reviewed the events of the previous Monday, considering how I could have handled the situation differently.

Several days that week, when it had been warmer, I had walked from Queen Margaret Hall where I lived to the campus atop Gilmorehill. The route took me through the Botanic Gardens. I crossed the Great Western Road by the BBC, ambled down Byres Road, then climbed the hill of University Avenue. Had I known we were being assigned our skeletons (or "skelingtons," as Dr. John Shaw-Dunn called them, accentuating every syllable), I should have taken the car.

Anatomy class enthralled me. Our muffled whispers around our cadaver echoed in the cavernous dissection hall. My team was from my end of the alphabet—Radford, Raeside, Roberts. Professor Scothorne had advised us to respect our assigned cadavers, all volunteers, unlike the bodies stolen from gravesites in the days of Burke and Hare in Edinburgh. At one end of the hall was a table covered with a sheet, under which were nestled human heads partially dissected. Someone had written a sign over the table, "This is the place to get ahead." Anatomy humor.

The skeletons came disassembled (apart from the hands and feet, which were articulated by wires), each packed in a wooden box about three feet long by a foot wide and a foot deep. I cautiously removed the ilium and turned the wing around to look at the pubis, the angle revealing whether my skelington was man or woman. Holding up the femur, I could see the ridges made by the muscular attachments and felt the smooth surface that would have abutted the articular cartilage of the femoral condyles.

Dr. Shaw-Dunn called out to us, " Okay, people, take your skelingtons home tonight. Keep them safe. They must be returned complete at the end of the fourth term."

When class was over, I picked up my box and set off for the walk back to hall. By the time I arrived at the bottom of the hill, the weight and bulk of my burden slowed my pace. I carried it every which way—on one shoulder, then the other, then resting on my hip—and, as I trudged heavy-footed into the park, dusk began to fall. Nearing the exit, on the wide path lined by benches, I heard a voice calling to me. Only after I turned round to spy the source of the noise did I realize what he'd said. "Look what I've got." And, indeed, what he had, the twentyish dark haired man in an overcoat, was an enormous erection, which he proceeded to wave at me with gusto.

When I got to this part of the saga, Mother had stopped drinking her tea, a McVities chocolate digestive poised in her hand on its way to her mouth. Dad had wandered in and sat down on the couch. All activity in the room had ceased.

"Then what did you do?" asked Mum.

"Well, I gripped my box tighter and scurried to the gate out of the gardens, which was only a few yards away. He got up from the bench and walked in the opposite direction." Mother's shoulders relaxed, and she wiped a crumb from her mouth. "The bugger," pronounced Dad. "Let me get my hands on the little perv."

I continued, "If I'd had any presence of mind, of course, I'd have put my box down, opened the lid, pulled out the skull, and said, 'And look what I've got.'"

Mum and Dad laughed, the tension broken. "Oh my," said Mum. "You're not as green as you're cabbage-looking." And with that enigmatic comment, she got up, holding her apron out horizontally to hold the crumbs till she could drop them outside. "Help me make the dinner."

Bonnets Over the Windmill

When my mother said, "Bonnets over the windmill," with her usual flourish, tossing an imaginary bonnet over a windmill only she could see, the idea it conjured up in my mind was one of great, unbridled, unexpurgated joy. At least this is how she seemed to use the expression. My mental picture was of a gowned mass of graduates tossing mortarboards aloft. That actual scene I did not come across in Glasgow, though, as Glasgow university graduates do not don mortarboards. Instead, the candidate for graduation kneels and is "capped," touched on the pate with a velvet cap, and the satin-lined hood is then thrown over robed shoulders before the graduate arises and is handed her parchment. But I had seen photographs and videos of the board-chucking ritual, so I knew it meant something wonderful and thrilling.

How wrong was I when I found out the likely meaning of the phrase.

Who says something like bonnets over the windmill, where did they hear it, who invented it? In my early fifties, recalling her use of the expression, I decided to do some research. I read the play *Bonnet Over the Windmill* by a fellow Lancashire native of my mother's, Dodie Smith. The play opened in London's West End in 1937. The main characters are three aspiring actresses, a journalist, a playwright, a theater mogul, a pianist, and a former variety performer turned landlady. The playwright, Kit, falls for one of the actresses, Janet, and takes her home to his windmill in Suffolk. His gift of white roses delivered to her the next day, leads us to the conclusion that Janet was deflowered the previous evening. Sex, in 1937, indeed.

Dorothy Gladys (Dodie) Smith and my mother had a common history—both grew up in Manchester and both had lost their fathers when very young. My mother was three when her dad died of tuberculosis; Dodie was two when her father passed away.

Dodie is best known as the author of children's books rather than as a playwright. Her bestseller *One Hundred and One Dalmatians* (1956) was three times adapted to film. The canine lead Pongo is based on her own dal, Pongo, her first of nine.

Although they lived in Manchester at the same time, I don't know if my mother ever met Dodie Smith in Mum's theatrical/artistic circles, which included playing with an amateur dramatic society. It's a question I would love to ask her. But I suspect she saw the play, as it likely ran in Dodie's hometown as well as London. When I reread the play some time later, another phrase in it struck me, occurring in an interchange between Kit and the theater mogul Sir Rupert Morellian. Kit asks Rupert to imagine the landlady's hair as, "as black as Egypt's night," not blonde. I had heard my mother use that description many a time during my formative years. I asked myself why the night in Egypt was any darker than anywhere else. My analytic brain concluded it had to be a part of Egypt away from a big city. But what about the stars studding the sky? Were there none? Despite the intrigue of the phrase, or perhaps because of it, "as black as Egypt's night" enthralled me.

Oscar Wilde refers to bonnets and mills in a couple of his works. In *The Picture of Dorian Gray* a lady says that if she had met Dorian earlier in life, she should have fallen madly in love with him and thrown her bonnet right over the mills for his sake. In *Lady Windermere's Fan* Mr. Dumby mentions that grandmothers threw their caps over the mills. So the phrase seems to imply sexual abandon. In a broader sense, bonnet throwing, to me, came to be a synonym for throwing caution to the wind.

Likely the phrase originates from *Don Quixote,* the seventeenth century novel by Cervantes, in which the eponymous hero tosses his hat over a windmill (which he sees as a giant) to challenge it to fight. Thus, it means to act in a deranged, reckless, or unconventional manner, which could indeed lead to sexual indiscretion.

But when I imagine Margery throwing an imaginary bonnet upwards, I prefer to think of prosperity, promise, and Dalmatian puppies, not promiscuity and profligacy.

Most often I understood my Mother's colorful expressions. This one still remains a bit of a mystery.

A Chance to Remember

A tinkling sound came from the teacup in Lady Margaret's hand as she stirred the steaming liquid in its fine porcelain crockery. She held both cup and spoon delicately. My parents and I had been invited to afternoon tea at Sir Tom and Lady Margaret's neat house on Lady Margaret Drive (named after one of the Bentincks, not our hostess). Tom Symington sat in an easy chair, his hands tenting fingertip to fingertip. We had been talking about my training and what I should do next. At the time, I was a senior house officer in the Surgical Specialties rotation in Glasgow. Turning his head to me, he said, "Well, Diane, if you want to specialize in cancer surgery, you really should go to America."

"Why do you say that?"

"I visited several cancer centers in the US as part of my purview as director of the Chester Beatty Cancer Research Institute. The training is excellent." His voice had a soft burr. Dad asked how long would I be away?

"Most fellowships are two years long, Sidney. How do you feel about that?"

Margaret interjected, "I'm sure they would miss her very much."

I put down my sandwich. "Well, if it's what I have to do to be well-trained, then let's look into it."

Mum asked, "Where are the best fellowships? Where should she go?"

"I met Edward Mirand at Roswell Park Memorial Institute in Buffalo. I really liked the program."

Professor Sir Thomas Symington was an esteemed researcher and teacher and I was fortunate to have his guidance. He grew up in Muirkirk, about thirty-five miles from Troon. Like my mother, he lost his father when he was three, not to tuberculosis, but to the influenza epidemic of 1918. Like my father, he came from a humble background—his father was

95

a coal miner. An accomplished athlete, Tom was advised to pursue a career as a professional soccer player rather than go to university. Fortunately, he did not heed that advice, instead entering Glasgow University where he obtained his biochemistry and medical degrees. His research into the functions of the adrenal gland elucidated the different zones of the adrenal cortex and the hormones produced by them. He was internationally renowned as a teacher and mentor, and, as evidenced by our conversation that afternoon in their living room, he took a great interest in young people and their careers. From 1970 until he retired, Professor Symington was director of the Chester Beatty in London. He suggested I write to Dr Mirand and go for a visit.

Margaret was a gracious and graceful hostess, offering freshly made sandwiches round the room. Dad had met Sir Tom at Royal Troon Golf Club, and they often played a round together, pulling their clubs behind them on carts as they walked the course. In Tom's obituary, written by his son Alan, we learned that Sir Tom was still playing off a handicap of fifteen at the age of eighty-seven. His other son, Robin, died of testicular cancer at the age of thirty, an event which devastated Margaret and Tom. In his memoir, *A Chance to Remember: My Life in Medicine*, published in 2003, Tom recounts how his son's death changed his life in that he switched his emphasis to terminal care. He and Margaret, also a physician, established the first Ayrshire Hospice, travelling throughout the county lecturing to raise funds. "He was very proud of the hospice and its achievements," according to his son Alan.

I'm sure it was through her association with Tom and Margaret that Mum decided to volunteer when the Hospice opened on Racecourse Road in Ayr in June 1989. Mum wrote to me in America in a firm hand on onion-skin Basildon Bond Airmail paper about her endeavors there. She explained that, since she was no longer driving, Sidney ferried her. "I help Dr. Bass, the medical director, by putting charts together for the new, incoming patients," she wrote. "I will not have nasturtiums cast on my reputation by saying I don't give back." Now, of course, she meant aspersions, and she knew this. It was just another of her intended Dogberryisms and made me smile all the way across the Atlantic.

Even after she no longer volunteered at the Hospice, she still helped raise funds. In another letter she included a snap of her dressed as Pierrot as part of a charity event, in another, fancy dress for a Teddy Bears Picnic fundraiser at Culzean. Her letters, while she could still see to write, were frequent. I treasured them.

I also treasure my copy of *A Chance to Remember*. Sir Tom had given me a typed pre-publication copy of the manuscript, and I was honored to read it. His influence on my career was immense; he truly was a mentor. In their later years, Mother and I visited the Symingtons when they were no longer living in their home. Even then, Sir Tom was engaged and inquisitive, asking me about where I was working and what research I was undertaking. Lady Margaret was most gracious, as always, causing me to think back to their cosy living room and the bell-like sound of the stirring spoon.

Margery during teacher training, Leeds, 1932

Sidney Radford in RAF flying uniform 1941

Sidney Radford in RAF uniform with Air Signaller brevet,
No. 1 Signals School, 1941. He qualified as an Air Gunner in 1942.

Margery and Sidney's wedding day

Sidney and Margery's wedding, 1946

Newlyweds

Margery and Sidney looking dapper

Margery with Diane, Hunter Crescent, 1959

On the beach, 1960

Sid and Margery on the beach

In the front garden with Margery's roses, Hunter Crescent 1961

In the back garden, Hunter Crescent, 1962

Margery and Sid at a Christmas party, Hunter Crescent

Sidney and Margery at the Marine Hotel dance

Margery with Pepe, Troon beach

Diane and Thomas the rabbit, Bentinck Drive

Diane kissing the Blarney Stone

Pepe in his tartan coat, Troon beach

Margery and Diane on the way to Speyside

Margery and Sidney lochside

Margery with her binos, Abernethy forest, Strathspey

Margery with Pepe in the back garden, Bentinck Drive

Margery, Diane, Auntie Joan, MBChB graduation, Glasgow, 1981

Concorde seen from Marine View Court

Marge and Sid on the balcony, Marine View Court

Diane and Margery at Niagara Falls

Margery during a visit to Buffalo, NY

Margery and Sidney, Sandilands

Margery and Sidney visit St. Louis

Margery and Troon lighthouse

Margery at Fullarton woods

Arran from Royal Troon, Sleeping Warrior

Bent trees, Bentinck Crescent

Margery, Sandilands

St. Ninian's Church, Troon

In the kitchen, Sandilands

Margery

Sidney Radford, Tailor, The Cross, Troon

Sidney sewing, Sandlands

South Bay, Troon, Marine Hotel in the distance

The Radford family, Sandilands, 1992

In loving memory of
SIDNEY and MARGERY RADFORD
From their daughter Diane

Inscription, the Bench, Troon promenade

Part Four

Marine View Court

My parents' home in Marine View Court was a modern flat with a wonderful view of the sea. They chose it for this and its central location, a stone's throw from Ayr Street and Troon Town Hall. From the balcony off the living room, they could see as far as Royal Troon Golf Club. More importantly for Mother, she could walk to the public library, a few hundred yards away on South Beach. I accompanied her on some of those library visits and noticed the transition over the years in her selection from regular print to large print editions.

Margery no longer had the same exuberant energy for gardening and condominium living allowed her to enjoy shrubbery and flowers tended by others.

There was a concrete streetlamp near the entrance to the driveway, which, until a metal one replaced it, bore a stripe of white paint from when I reversed my two-tone Hillman Avenger into it.

Dad could easily drive to the golf club from the covered parking area. It was a great abode for both of them, and the last home in which I resided in Scotland while I was a registrar (senior resident) in surgery at Crosshouse Hospital, outside Kilmarnock.

Taxi-Parade

Once a year the esplanade at Troon becomes festive and colorful. The occasion? The summer day-at-the-beach organized by the Glasgow Taxi Drivers for children with special needs. We had a prime view of events from the flat in Marine View Court, from which we could see the expanse of the South Beach and promenade.

Since 1945 Glasgow cabbies have been giving up a day of income for this much-appreciated day. They don fancy dress...and so do their usually plain black cabs. Over the years the designs have changed to suit contemporary themes. After all, there wasn't always a Sponge Bob, but perennial favorites include swashbuckling pirates, Disney characters, the Wizard of Oz, heroes from children's books, and clowns with balloons everywhere.

In 2013, the prize for best-decorated taxi went to a Lego-themed design. In 1988, a taxi transformed into a spaceship, completely covered in aluminum foil, won the award. The drivers spend up to a week decorating their vehicles. In 2015, one cab was totally engulfed by a layer of soft toys.

The taxicab convoy starts in the center of Glasgow, often by Kelvingrove Park, led off by bagpipers. With horns tooting, they make their way down the A77. It's quite a sight, guaranteed to make the evening news.

Following the thirty-five-mile road trip, the convoy arrives in Troon for a parade down Portland Street, again led by bagpipers, then turns onto Ayr Street at The Cross in front of Dad's former shop, before finally parking on the esplanade.

From our vantage point on the balcony one summer's day in the early eighties we watched as the taxis lined the esplanade and delivered their precious, excited cargo—kids who had been picked up from Assisted Living Support Schools all over Glasgow for this supremely special day.

As two taxi drivers (dressed as Tom and Jerry) explained to a cow, AKA Colin Stone, of Scottish Television's Riverside Show, "Sadly, for many of these kids, it's the only day of the year they'll get to the beach."

As we watched the bustling scene below us, Mum said, "Let's go down there, get in the thick of it." I happily agreed. Strolling along the prom, we heard shrieks of joy from beaming kids. The esplanade was so busy, we had to dodge balloons and loosely held teetering, dripping ice cream cones in danger of losing their rapidly liquefying contents. "Press on, McDuff," urged Mum, leading the way through the throngs. Like many of the Troon residents, the "Taxis to Troon" day is as much fun for us as it is for the taxi drivers and children. It's a day of joy, and only a crusty curmudgeon could not be swept up in it all.

We rested for a while on the esplanade wall and watched the pony rides. Deciding to sit, Mum quickly got up again and looked behind her, saying, "Now there's a sign of an early spring," noting that she had sat on a child's Dinky toy car. She patted her bottom, shifted the toy, and sat down again gingerly. Thankfully, the weather held: a sunny day at the beach, perfect for the jugglers, musicians, and clowns to entertain; perfect for the face painters, magicians, ice cream vendors, and pony handlers, all of whom donated their talents and wares.

In that same STV interview Colin asked the Cat in the Hat, who stood in front of his Dr. Seuss-themed cab, why he kept coming back, year after year for twenty-seven years. "It's heartwarming," said the Cat, his answer echoed by other drivers. "It's the one day of the year we give something back to the kids. It's humbling."

"It's all about the kids," said another driver. Had Mum seen the interview, I can envision her reaction. She would have smiled and said, "It warms the cockles of my heart."

There Was a War On

Mother was busying herself around the flat, duster in hand, and as she often did, she sang. This time a rendition of "Yes! We Have No Bananas." She paused, rag in hand and turned to me, "You know we didn't have any bananas during the war. We didn't have a lot of things." She put down the Pledge. "In fact, we didn't have much to eat at all—everything was rationed, food, clothing, fuel. People in 1984 have no idea how lucky they have it." She waved her duster for emphasis, "Just. No. Idea."

And she was probably right. I don't think we who were never there can ever appreciate what it was like. I think we can only imagine and read accounts recorded by those who lived through it. Dad left his position as manager of Hector Powe Tailoring on Regent Street in London to join the forces soon after Chamberlain declared war with Germany on Sept. 3, 1939. Mum had graduated from teacher training college in Leeds and was working as an elementary school teacher.

"I think I told you I had to save up coupons for my wedding dress." She had indeed, many times, but I never was bored by her stories. The tale of their wedding was true romance. Mum and Dad met and dated in the early 1940s, and then lost touch. She became engaged to another military man, but it broke off; she would never tell me why. When I asked, using one of her many quaint sayings, all she would say was, "All cats are grey in the dark," then continued with whatever she was doing—whether it was washing the dishes, her hands clad in colorful rubber gauntlets, or preparing Pepe's gourmet meals. The rest was for me to infer.

My parents' romance rekindled after a chance encounter on a Manchester street. Sid exited a tobacconist carrying a pack of Players—the cigarettes all the flyboys smoked—almost bumped into my mother, and all at once they were talking again, laughing, he in his blue uniform with the winged AG brevet on the chest for Air Gunner, with his North Africa tan and dimpled chin. Mum recounted many of these memories when we took our walks together. The Romance of Margery and Sidney—Sid and Marge together again—went the storyline. As we were linked arm in arm against the gusting wind, with the gulls cawing overhead, I felt her arm tense as she squeezed mine to emphasize a point, "He was so dashing—broad shoulders, narrow waist, his back an inverted triangle."

She released my arm in order to trace his silhouette in the air with her hands. Dad may never have had the broadest shoulders or the narrowest waist, but he was an award-winning tailor and cutter, who could render to any man the finest physique, so he was able to alter his own uniform accordingly. Margery said, "He was always the smartest, the most sartorial. I can't stand a sloppy uniform." So it was his dress sense, plus his dimpled chin and tan that won her over.

Mum taught at Briscoe Lane Primary in Newton Heath, a suburb of Manchester, when war broke out. Manchester was a prime target for the Luftwaffe because of its heavy industry, airplane factories, and the Manchester Ship Canal. Trafford Park, in the western part of the city, was the production site for Rolls Royce Merlin engines, which powered the Spitfire and Hurricane fighter planes, the de Havilland Mosquito and Lancaster bombers.

Anticipating heavy bombing, the evacuation of children out of the cities to safer rural homes, their "host homes," started before war began. In the first four days of September 1939 nearly three million people were evacuated throughout the country. The majority were schoolchildren; however, the BBC reported that among them were 100,000 teachers and some parents. Among the evacuees was my cousin Barry, Uncle Les's son, who was aged nine at the time.

The city of Manchester sustained its worst bombing just before Christmas 1940. The Blitz on Manchester began in August 1940, and aerial attacks took place throughout the war—high explosives, incendiary bombs, and later V1 flying bombs. Whenever Mum recounted stories of the raids, her eyes misted over and her voice shook. "The sirens, the fleeing to the air raid shelter, the gas masks, the sound of the bombs. You'd never know if you would live or die." She paused, and then carried on. "The search lights, the blackouts, and antiaircraft guns. It was so hard for me because your grandmother had had a stroke and was in a Bath chair. Imagine getting her out of the building in a hurry." She shook her head as she reminisced.

She told of friends of the family, who had an air-raid shelter in their garden. The mother took her children to the shelter at the start of one raid. When it ended and everyone went back to their homes, Mum saw the tragedy. "It was a direct hit, the house was spared, the shelter fragmented to rubble," she remembered.

When Pam and I visited Manchester some seventy years after the blitz, we saw the phoenix-like transformation of the city: previously embattled, a beleaguered, rubble-strewn bombers' target, it is now a forward-thinking metropolis. The smoke stacks and drab huddled stick-people which characterized the city in L. S. Lowry's paintings have been replaced by elegant office buildings alongside the Salford docks and bustling laden shoppers in the pedestrian precincts. From our hotel, named after the painter, it is a short walk to the city center over Calatrava Trinity Bridge across the sparkling waters of the River Irwell.

As Pam and I walked towards St Ann's church, past the square with lampposts festooned with flower boxes overflowing with color, I recalled my mum's description of her wedding there. "It took a while to save up those clothing coupons." She added, "Of course, HRH Princess Elizabeth had to save coupons for her dress when she married Philip a year after our wedding." No doubt the Princess required more coupons as her frock was embroidered with thousands of pearls in a motif of flowers with anchors to represent Philip's naval background. The government allowed the Princess 200 extra coupons towards her trousseau; the regular folk were allotted thirty-six coupons a year for all their clothes. But the country needed something fancy like a royal wedding, after the gloom of war. The cities were being rebuilt, although clothes rationing would continue till 1949. Mum's was a plain dress, no embroidered pearls.

"Why no white?" I asked.

"I was too old and had seen too much," she said matter-of-factly.

I prefer to believe there was a shortage of white fabric.

St Ann's is a magnificent building, completed in 1712, made from huge local red Collyhurst sandstone blocks. Over the centuries, as the soft bricks required repair, sandstone was brought in from other parts of the North country—yellow-grey stone from Darley Dale; pink from Hollington, Staffordshire; dark red from Runcorn in Cheshire; and pale brown from Parbold, Lancashire—each repair adding to a jaunty patchwork.

Pam and I turned onto Deansgate, then St. Ann Street; and as we neared the church, I recognized the eclectic façade, the Corinthian pilasters standing sentry to the doorway, so familiar to me from my parents' wedding album. To the right of the grand door, at the base of the church tower, was a flower stall, adding a splash of color to the scene. Fidgeting at the entrance that summer's day was a wedding party. I worried; maybe we would not be able to see inside the church if the ceremony was about to take place. I asked a kind looking gent if we could go in, "since my parents were married here in 1946."

"My brother is getting married here in an hour. If you don't take long, go in and have a look before the guests come."

That day in October 1946 must have been chilly; the photos outside the church show my great-aunt in fur, keeping her collar warm against her neck. Pressed inside the album's pages lay the cutting from the *Manchester Guardian* (now just *The Guardian*) describing their wedding: "The groom has flown in over 70 operational sorties...The bride was attired in a gown of ice-blue, with a veil and head-dress of orange blossom...A reception was held at the Grand Hotel, after which the couple left for London."

The album's black and white images did not prepare me for the magnificence of the church's interior. At the far end of the aisle is the renowned large curved apse, beneath three huge panels of stained glass. The choir rehearsed its repertoire for the service, their voices filling the space. Adorning the end of each pew hung gossamer-white chiffon ribbons. Flanking the kneelers for the bride and groom stood bouquets of white roses. No chiffon ribbons for Marge and Sid, of course; not enough ration coupons, and besides, Margery would tell you, "There was a war on."

I inhaled the sacred space, revered the memory, and remembered the couple that knelt on those altar kneelers there all those years before.

Part Five

Sandilands

When my parents moved into Sandilands, it was owned by the adjoining church, St. Ninian's, and the apartments rented out to parishioners. The property comprised a row of townhomes built around 1910, with gardens to the rear and a vast lawn in front, separated from the sidewalk of Bentinck Drive by a wall about four and a half feet high. A row of garages was detached from the building, to the northwest side of the property.

My parents had pragmatically decided they needed to own fewer possessions, including a house, deciding to rent instead. Their unit had a large combined living and dining room downstairs, with a cloakroom and the kitchen on the same level. Upstairs were a bathroom and four bedrooms, two of which served as studies. Their friends the Frews lived a couple of doors down.

By this time, I had moved to the US to continue my studies and practice medicine. One afternoon, on one of my transatlantic visits home, Dad, then in his late seventies, took me upstairs to his study. Hers was her artist's studio: bright, open, with a table a mishmash of brushes, tubes of paint, and works in progress, and a view of the sea. His was to the front of the house; I could see through the window the daffodils in bloom in the flowerbeds below. Certificates awarded him by Tailor and Cutter magazine hung on the walls, and although he had long since retired, on a small table in the middle of the room, rested a Singer sewing machine, for minor alterations. Against the wall stood an old bureau, which had moved from house to house with them. Scratched in places, its claw feet worn down from years of standing, it held the Family Papers.

Dad opened the bottom drawer. "I want to show you this now. You need to know where these things are." What he didn't say, but which I knew he meant, was that he didn't know how long he would have his faculties, when he would no longer remember where things were, or would no longer be able to tell me.

He lifted out flat filing sheaves, bank statements, stock certificates, and information on the annuities they held with Building Societies, explaining each item. He looked at me quizzically; I could see the arcus senilis around his irises, a sign of aging. I nodded. I could no longer speak. My throat was tight. I willed myself not to let my chin quiver.

He hugged me and pecked my cheek; we went downstairs hand in hand.

The Sleeping Warrior

It's called the Sleeping Warrior, the outline traced by the mountaintops of the Isle of Arran, across the bay from Troon. To the North his hair splays out behind his massive head; his pointed toes lie at the South end of the island, pushing skyward. The highest point of the range, the peak of Goatfell, is the hilt of his sword, resting on his chest. Sunset puts him in silhouette, painting him a dark purple against the salmon sky. He is a constant.

My mother never tired of him. We would be linked arm in arm on our walks, dodging the seaweed underfoot, a misplaced step causing a "pop." The sea had sculpted the banks of the temporary streams that we crossed with larger strides. Gulls cawed overhead, gliding on the thermals, and a few tuxedo-clad oystercatchers paddled along the shoreline, occasionally bobbing their orange beaks in search of food.

As we looked west towards Arran, the lighthouse of Lady Isle blinked at us in the foreground. On our left, the Heads of Ayr formed the boundary for the South end of the bay. The island of Ailsa Craig rose steeply out of the horizon.

It was a view we both revered. My mother, a poetry lover, took her stance on the wet sand and recited her favorite lines of British Poet Laureate John Masefield:

I must go down to the seas again, to the lonely sea and the sky,
And all I ask is a tall ship and a star to steer her by...

The wind that would have powered that tall ship caught Margery's head square, billowing it like a sail. She pulled the ties of her scarf tighter, flattening a newly coiffed perm, her hair tinted "Intoxicating Ivory." She took a deep breath of the tangy air, and we ambled over the ribbed sand, turning our backs to the warrior, the sentry to the lonely sea and the sky.

Patter-Merchant

Mother's Day in the UK falls on a different day than in the US. This was a bone of contention between my mother and me, for I always got it wrong once I moved to the US in 1985. It seemed no matter how hard I tried, I either called late or missed it altogether. The barrage of TV advertisements, newspaper ads, and Hallmark store banners in the States all told me, in all-too-clamant tones, that Mother's Day came on the second Sunday in May. A true statement, of course, for a host of other countries as well as the US, such as Australia, Canada, Switzerland, even Samoa.

Mothering Sunday, as it's called in the UK, follows the Anglican Liturgical calendar and falls on the fourth Sunday in Lent. The Nigerians and Irish also celebrate Mothering Sunday on this day. Easter is a moveable feast, changing the date of Mothering Sunday to a day most often in March. It is never, never, not ever in May. So it never coincides with Mother's Day in the US. Basically, call me toast as far as remembering the vagaries of Mother's Day.

We'd be on our usual Sunday afternoon transatlantic call from St. Louis to Troon—2 p.m. my time was 8 p.m. hers. After the chitchat about our week she'd ask,

"Have you forgotten?"

Well, obviously, whatever it was (and I had a twinkling of a notion what it was), I had forgotten, but I tried to feign ignorance.

"Forgotten what?" I tried my best to sound innocent.

"Mother's Day. You forgot Mother's Day."

Once again, I found myself in deep kaka.

"Mother's Day isn't until May; I have your card already, ready to send."

"We had Mothering Sunday services at St. Ninian's today, so it's today."

There was no good recovery from this one, but I thought I had nothing to lose.

"As far as I'm concerned, it's Mother's Day every day."

Now there is some truth to that, when we look at how Mother's Day is celebrated around the world, because it could always be Mother's Day somewhere: In Norway, it's the second Sunday in February; in early March (the eighth), Mothers are recognized in Albania, Macedonia, and Serbia, to name a few. The vernal equinox, March 21, is the day motherhood is celebrated in Egypt, Lebanon, Saudi Arabia, and many other Arab countries. The Armenians choose April 7. On the Iberian Peninsula, it's the first Sunday in May. In Mexico it's May 10. In Paraguay Mothers are celebrated on May 15, the same day as Dia de la Patria. The French honor Mother's Day on the last Sunday in May, or the first Sunday in June, depending on when Pentecost falls. In Kenya, it's the last Sunday in June. In Thailand it's August 12, the birthday of Queen Sirikit. The Argentines have Dia de la Madre on the third Sunday of October, the Russians honor motherhood on the last Sunday in November, and the Indonesians, December 22.

So I did have a point, in retrospect.

"You are such a chancer, Diane Radford, a real patter-merchant," she said, using the Scottish idiom for one with the gift of the gab. According to family legend, this was first bestowed on me one summer during our family vacation to Ireland. With my waist secure in the arms of the attendant and my skirted legs covered with a blanket to prevent unwitting exposure, I arched my back, leaned backwards and kissed the rather slimy surface of the Blarney Stone. Voila—instantaneous loquacity.

I knew Mum and I were reconciled then, that I was forgiven. She chuckled. "All right then, I'll give you that one."

I was golden.

Over the years, I tried; I really tried to remember the correct day. Some years I sent a card that arrived in between, late for one and early for the other. There were years I sent only a card for UK Mother's Day (when I had a UK calendar at home), and other years I sent a card for U.S. Mother's Day only. I got the most points when I sent a card for both—Mother's Day in stereo.

Father's Day falls on the same day in the UK and the US, thank God, the third Sunday in June. If you live in the Antipodes—in Australia and New Zealand—however, it's the first Sunday in September. It was easier for Dad. I'd send a card, make a phone call, and say, "I love you, Dad."

"I love you, too, my poppet," he would reply. Easy, peasy.

A Unit of Measurement

When my parents lived at Sandilands, they were fortunate enough to have Mary and Alastair Frew living a few doors down. Alastair no longer had an aviary on his property, but his daughter Joy and her husband Derek had one at their home in the neighboring village of Dundonald. Every so often Al would stop by with a special gift for Mum and Dad, quail's eggs. He would be beaming as he handed them over to Margery with a chuckle. I think about Uncle Al on the anniversary of D-Day every year.

The sixth of June 2014 marked the seventieth anniversary of D-Day, the landings by Allied Forces on the beaches of Normandy, France. Those landings began Operation Overlord, the Battle of Normandy; the mission to free occupied France. On that day in 1944 160,000 Allied troops crossed the English Channel, the biggest armada the world had ever seen. The sounds of the bombardment could be heard six miles inland.

But the landings did not end that day; they continued for twenty-five days. Among those later arriving troops were the Seaforth Highlanders, leaping out of vessels into the cold waves coming to shore on Sword Beach. One Highlander would have stood out among them, a towering man, 6'3" from top of pate to sole of boot: Alastair Frew.

In June 1944 Sid was stationed with the RAF in Masirah, Oman, serving as rear gunner on what was to become his favorite aircraft, the Wellington XIII. Sid and Al, who became lifelong friends, did not meet during the war, though. It wasn't until the '50s, when their wives shared adjoining classrooms in Milngavie. When Margery chatted with Al, she had to crane her neck because of his height. Alastair sometimes absent-mindedly rubbed his hands, the right hand smoothing over the truncated left palm, where the little finger used to be. She was so impressed by his height, to her he was a unit of measurement. I'd ask her to tell me how tall a tree was, and she'd say, "About ten Uncle Alastairs."

The Seaforth Highlanders were part of the 46th (Highland) Brigade, which in turn was part of the 15th Scottish Division. One of General Bernard Montgomery's prime objectives in Operation Epsom was to encircle the town of Caen. Whoever had control of the high ground outside Caen had control of the land around it. That high ground was known as Hill 112—the notorious Hill 112. The 15th Scottish Division, among them Al Frew, began the offensive at 7:30 a.m. on June 26, 1944. Heavy fighting raged for six weeks for control of Hill 112, from June to August, and involved 63,000 men.

Al was one of the thousands of casualties on battle-torn Hill 112, sustaining numerous gunshot wounds to his limbs. The story goes that he got a message through to Mary that his pinkie had been shot off. Something was lost in translation, however, for Mary thought they'd never be able to have children. Following recuperation at Hairmyres Hospital and to Mary's relief, this proved not to be the case.

We were all thankful for Uncle Al, for kind, jovial, impressive, bird-loving, and incredibly brave and heroic Uncle Al—a unit of measurement.

Funny Ha-Ha or Funny Peculiar

"Panto tickets!"

The shriek echoed round the hallway. "Where are the panto tickets?" Mother cried, her hands like the blades of a bread maker rummaging through her voluminous handbag. Dad looked up from his sewing, pausing mid threading motion, the tweed jacket over his knee and the errant button pirouetting down the thread towards the jacket cuff.

"Hell if I know," he declared. "Last time I saw them, they were on the kitchen table."

"Well, Sidney Radford, they're not there now, so that observation doesn't help me. But this is really funny; I saw them earlier today."

"Funny ha-ha or funny peculiar?" I said it before Dad did, both of us knowing this as one of her catch phrases.

"Funny peculiar, of course," pushing her specs up on her nose as she spoke.

I knew what she'd do next. I'd seen it a thousand times. Kneeling, she spread the pages of *The Telegraph* on the ground and upended her handbag, shaking it until it appeared nothing else could be secreted within. Next came the spreading motion, palms down over the contents, moving them so they didn't overlay and each one could be seen plainly.

Next, she started replacing the objects in her purse, picking each up carefully, studying it, and putting it away in its designated spot. I saw her find her compact, change purse, wallet with membership cards, her Kleenex. But no tickets for the Christmas pantomime at the Gaiety Theatre.

"Maybe they were filed under P for Panto?" I suggested, knowing that she had some sort of system for her belongings, however obscure that may be to an observer.

She sighed. "I know they are somewhere *safe*."

"Yes, very safe, indeed. No tickets going to escape here," I commented. "How about I go upstairs and look in your bedroom?" I could see there was very little left to go back into its cavernous leather home, so I had to think of other possibilities.

What we were all hunting for were the tickets to the only-the-British-could-do-it entertainment—the pantomime. A combination of vaudeville, musical, comedy, slapstick, and drag show, pantomime first became popular in the UK in the 1800s and was quickly a Christmas tradition and a bit of a gender-bender with the leading "boy" being a girl and the "dame" a guy in drag. Commonly based on a nursery rhyme, fable, or children's story, the pantomimes are interactive, with frequent exchanges between the main players and the audience, and are played to the whole family.

I climbed the stairs and entered their bedroom, the room overlooking the semicircular driveway at Sandilands, from which Mum could see the daffodils in the spring and watch the rooks hopping clumsily for the torn-up pieces of old bread she had left for them. Tucked in the frame of her vanity mirror was the envelope containing the tickets. By the time I descended the stairs, Margery's bag was back in ship-shape condition. I flourished the tickets. "Found them! Tucked in your mirror."

"Well, of course," said Mum. "That's where they were last." Dad looked up from his sewing, and I caught him rolling his eyes in disbelief.

"It's tonight, right?"

"Yes, Sid. A special treat for Diane's trip home." Following my move to the States, I rarely went home for Christmas, call schedules often precluding it, so this visit was a special treat for them and me.

That evening I drove us up to Ayr for the performance. Mum chatted about watching the pantomime in Manchester when she was a child, remembering being taken by her mother and aunt. I found a parking space designated disabled and placed Margery's card on the dash, then helped her out of the car, protecting her head with my hand. Both of my parents were a bit fragile by this time.

The Gaiety Theatre, on Carrick Street, was just a short walk from the car. After opening its doors in 1902, it became the largest performance venue between Glasgow and the border. Famous entertainers have graced its stage, including Sir Harry Lauder and the comedian Johnny Beattie. At one time, annual audiences numbered over 80,000 entertained by more than 220 shows.

Like a phoenix from the ashes, it was rebuilt following two fires: one within a year of opening and the other in 1955. For forty-eight years, from 1925 to 1973, the theatre was owned by the Popplewell family, who then sold it to the local Council in 1974. Following a steady decline in audiences, it closed in 2009. A valiant fundraising effort by local residents and the charity the Ayr Gaiety Partnership enabled the venue to reopen in December 2012 for forty sell-out performances of the panto *Cinderella*. It has remained open ever since.

I do not recall which panto was playing that evening I steered my parents into the lobby and offered the tickets to the waist-coated usher: *Jack and the Beanstalk, Sleeping Beauty, Mother Goose, Puss in Boots, Aladdin* or any one of a dozen other titles. Whichever it was, it provided a night of fun: songs, colorful costumes, double entendres, and a lot of "Oh no he didn't," and the response shouted back by the audience, "Oh yes he did." But first, there was the issue of the tickets.

The usher started to tear the stubs when he paused, took another look, shook his head and said, "These were for last night's show."

"No, they can't be," pleaded Margery. "We've been looking forward to this for months." He could see her crestfallen look and took in the scene: two elderly (apparently forgetful) parents with their only child.

"Let me talk to the manager." We were guided to a bench on one side of the lobby, while he sought a remedy for our predicament. Five minutes later he returned, successful in finding three seats for that night's almost sold out performance. New tickets in hand we were accompanied into the rococo-style performance hall by another attendant. Our seats were not together: Dad was shown into a plush red velvet-covered seat behind one of the columns to the side of the auditorium, while Mum and I sat at the end of the back row—no column obscuring our view at least. For the next ninety minutes we joined the fun, laughed till we either cried or snorted, clapped, and shouted out back to the panto "dame."

At the end of the show, as the principal "boy" was taking her bow, Mum reached into her handbag for a tissue to dab her eyes (filed under K for Kleenex, of course). "Oh my, I laughed so much I can hardly breathe," she said. Soon our little family was reunited in the lobby, and as we drove home, we talked about the show. Remembering the panto dame with his petticoats and heavy makeup, Mum declared about the evening's performance, "It was both funny ha-ha *and* funny peculiar."

Part Six

Dallas Place, Princes Square, and Westbank

The time Margery and Sidney resided in each of their last three homes was relatively short, for example, only a year each at Princes Square and Westbank. Dallas Place and Princes Square are "age exclusive housing" for those sixty and above, with Dallas Place providing "amenity housing" and Princes Square "sheltered housing." Sheltered has all the features of amenity, plus a community lounge for socializing and a shared laundry. Both types are supervised by a housing manager, once called a warden, a term that always made me cringe when Margery used it, as I likened it to being confined to a penitentiary. For obvious reasons, the term is no longer used. Residents are expected to be fairly independent, as staff do not provide nursing or domestic services, nor cook meals or do shopping for residents, although the units are fitted with alarm systems allowing residents to summon help in an emergency with a pull cord in every room. Both are well located, Dallas Place being half a mile from town (but near to a bus stop), and Princes Square only 100 yards from the town center, making it easy walking, even for Mum.

The wait for my parents to enter age exclusive housing seemed excessively long, years in fact. One day when I was home from the States and staying with them at Sandilands, as I took the stairs beside Mum while she ascended on the recently-installed chair lift, I asked her, "Why's it taking so long?" Her hand came off the lever, stopping the machine, and as she turned her head to me, she said, "Because, my dear Diane, the accommodations are only One Bedroom, and I no longer wish to share a room with Your Father. I keep taking our names off the Council's waiting list."

Ah-ha.

So we had a talk about what they really needed, and how by then they'd been married over fifty years, and couldn't she just deal with whatever friction was going on between them since they'd be safer elsewhere. I suspect, though I did not recognize it at the time, my dad was becoming more argumentative as he aged. The next day she conceded, and I was allowed to go to the Council offices and lobby on their behalf. Months later, they moved to Dallas Place.

One day in 2004 my mother had to pull the emergency cord in the flat at Princes Square; Dad had collapsed. They would never return to independent living.

Westbank is one of the nursing homes in Troon, located on Titchfield Road. It's red sandstone and pebble-dash façade overlook the South Bay. In the near distance are the parking lot where the old open-air swimming pool used to be and the manicured Italian Gardens. In the far distance is Royal Troon Golf Club, and in between, the gentle curve of the bay and the broad beach. When Mum and I researched nursing homes while Dad was hospitalized, we visited not only Westbank, with its commanding view, but also the Sun Court, Belhaven, and Dundonald. The Sun Court also faces the sea, and overlooks the fairways and broom of Royal Troon. It used to be the Sun Court Hotel, where Dad hosted Rotary Club dinners when he was club president. Belhaven is also well positioned across the road from Royal Troon Clubhouse. However, access to the golf course was no longer a concern for Mum and Dad. Dundonald House, in the picturesque, charming village of Dundonald, lies more inland. The ruins of Dundonald Castle, on the grounds of which we used to take Pepe for walks, are nearby.

After our reconnaissance mission, Mother decided, of course, she had to be *"by the sea."* She loved Westbank, and more importantly, it had rooms available—*two* rooms.

Westbank was the last home of their peripatetic around Troon housing.

Elegant Sufficiency

As my Dad became more infirm, he was unable to join Mum and me for dinners out, and dining out was one of Margery's favorite activities. She had a cadre of restaurants she preferred: the Lookout by the Marina, Highgrove House on Dundonald Hill, Cecchini's on Portland Street, and the Maharani for Indian. She loved the Lookout because one wall was all aquaria. Her eyesight failing by this time, I would describe to her all the multi-colored fish, how they looked, how they swam, how they darted and gleamed. I would tell her about the yachts moored in the marina and about the comings and goings of the boats and those who owned them. Whichever our venue, however, our process was the same.

When we arrived, I would guide her to her seat and bring the table forward for her. Some people would stare because of the white stick, stares which fortunately, Margery couldn't see. I'd read off the menu items, skipping those I knew were never going to be considered. If Highgrove, she'd settle on a melon dish for starters and chicken for her main course. If Indian food, we'd start with pakora and then enjoy chicken tikka masala. When the food arrived, I'd cut it up for her and describe the topography of her plate: chicken at six o'clock, rice at nine, chutney at twelve and so on. If she failed to spear something with her fork, but didn't know it, I'd line up the next bite. If I saw her right hand reach out for her wine glass, I'd gently fold her fingers around the stem so she could raise it to her lips.

During the meal we'd chat about what was going on with Dad, how things were.

At the end of the meal she'd often say, "Ahhhh, that was wonderful. I am replete." She'd push back from the table.

"Have you had enough to eat?" I'd ask.

"I have had an elegant sufficiency. Any more would be sheer gluttony on my part." She'd pat her tummy. I'd help her with her coat before bringing the car curbside, her disabled card on the dash, then guide her to her seat.

"Where are we eating tomorrow?" she'd ask.

Old Buggerlugs

On the wall of his room at Westbank hung the painting that I had bought Dad for his ninetieth birthday—Wellington bombers under attack over the dark waters of the English Channel. He often told me that, despite the combat, he loved those wartime years because he flew so often. Aviation thrilled him.

I recall once standing with Dad on the balcony at Marine View Court looking out over Troon bay. The amber evening light reflected off his specs, and his thick, wavy hair—already on its way to pure white—stirred in the breeze coming off the ocean. I joined him that evening in the early 1980s, and as we scanned the sky, we saw Concorde coming in for a landing at Prestwick, four miles away to the south, its sleek shape silhouetted against the glowing clouds. "Looks like a paper dart, perfect shape for flying," he murmured.

"Yes, ideal streamlined shape. Least resistance."

"Think we'll ever fly in her?"

"Who knows? But what an experience that would be."

Dad nodded in agreement as we watched her descend, her articulated nose down. The nose had to be down on takeoff and landing for the pilot to see the runway. Mum came to join us out on the balcony. "What are you and Old Buggerlugs up to, out here in the breeze while I'm getting the tea ready?" To answer her I pointed out over the bay.

"Ah, Concorde pilot training." She squeezed Dad's hand, and the three of us observed the plane in the distance.

One of only two supersonic passenger planes, the other made by the Russians, Concorde was a joint venture between the UK and France. Concorde first flew in 1969 and entered commercial service in 1976. She reached a height of 60,000 feet, with a cruising speed of 1,350 mph. There was nothing between the plane and space—and the universe beyond. Only the most seasoned and best British Airways pilots ever captained her. They trained at the Ayrshire coastal town of Prestwick, its runways famous for being free of fog compared to all other airports in Britain. Thus Dad, Mum, and I were treated to this amazing sight on a regular basis, as the pilots familiarized themselves with the craft.

Dad loved to fly; he loved planes and all things related to aviation. Whenever we flew as a family, Dad favored the window seat and liked to provide a running commentary on the flight. "Undercarriage just came down," he'd say, as we neared our destination. Sid loved watching planes arrive and take off, imagining who the passengers were coming to visit, who would be there to hug them hello and goodbye. In the 1960s and 1970s there was a rooftop viewing area at Prestwick Airport, perfect for plane watching. Dad and I, he armed with his binos and me with my notebook, would spend a weekend afternoon spotting aircraft. Then the planes were BEA and BOAC with a few British Caledonian, all airlines later consumed under the British Airways marquee. I'd note the airline, type of plane, the livery, and serial numbers.

Sid's love of planes going back to his childhood led him to volunteer for the RAF in the early years of WWII. His brother Jack joined the Navy, his sister Nancie labored in the local munitions factory, and his oldest brother Les served in the Army—a whole generation of Radfords for the war effort. Trained as a rear gunner and wireless operator in the RAF in the early 1940s, Dad crewed in over twenty varieties of aircraft during the war. More than once I had leafed through his RAF logbook, its spine buckled with age, in which he listed, in neat capitals and elegant fountain pen cursive, all of his sorties: which plane, what model number, the squadron, the pilot, the mission, the outcome, the hours flown.

Beside one of his entries he had a newspaper clipping, since browned, but still legible, about the pilot: "He has shown exceptional courage, and his list of destroyed aircraft now totals five."

Sid served in North Africa and the Middle East. The names of the bases are familiar to us now, as they were outposts for the allied forces in the Iraq war—Baghdad, Basrah, and Habbaniya. He would tell me with pride about the skirmish with the Italians (allied with Germany), the crash in the desert, the broken foot, and the injury to his leg from twisted metal as the fuselage hit the sand dunes.

It's a wonder he lived. But, of course, he had to live; he was yet to marry my mother. A cursory inspection of his thigh revealed a twelve-inch scar from the deep laceration. He could never run well after that; it was a jerky, listing motion. With pride he'd show me the small, creased snap he took of Churchill, the Prime Minister, when he came to the desert to boost morale, iconic cigar jutting from pursed lips.

Sid was a rear gunner, a "tail-end Charlie." His position on the plane suffered from the highest mortality rate. He crewed in many planes after his initial gunner training, but his favorite craft of all aircraft he flew was the Wellington bomber, the "Wimpy."

He was assigned to Wellingtons in the last couple of years of the war as part of Coastal Command, protecting Atlantic convoys, patrolling for the U-boats that hunted the merchant vessels carrying vital supplies to the threatened island. His plane was always at risk from the Luftwaffe fighters, who could come up the rear to take out the rear gunner, then the aircraft and the rest of the crew. The rear gunner's turret was a perspex (plexiglas) dome, unheated, numbingly cold, bitter, bitter to the bone. He sat alone, isolated from the other crew members, just the gunner and his guns.

In the summer of 2010, Pam and I toured the aviation museums of Britain to see examples of those planes in which my Dad flew. By then, there were only two Wellington bombers left in existence. The one normally on display in the Royal Air Force Museum was under restoration and not on view. The other one was at Brooklands Museum in Surrey.

Brooklands only houses aircraft that were manufactured there, such as the Wellington. One of the other famous vehicles made there was the Concorde—the articulated nose and delta tail fashioned at Brooklands, the chassis in France. In the back of a huge Bellman hanger stood the only remaining Wimpy to have seen service; the sole survivor left intact of the over 11,000 Wellingtons produced in World War II. I took in the aluminum frame with the thin covering of painted "doped" Irish linen stretched across it. Exposed was the geodesic Barnes Wallis design, so strong that a plane totally shot up and burned could still limp home. The left propeller was mangled; the other prop was relatively unscathed. This aircraft was discovered on the bottom of Loch Ness in 1985 by an

American underwater research team, "Nessie" hunters. I walked to the back of the aircraft and stared into the cramped rear gun turret, with its twin 0.303in (7.7mm) Browning belt-fed machine guns.

"Engine failure," intoned the guide who had observed my fascination, anticipating my question about the aircraft's fate. "The intact propeller was not turning when she hit the surface of the Loch. The other was going full speed; hence, all the damage to it."

"Were there any survivors?" I asked, my throat tight.

"The crew survived bar one, the rear gunner. He could not get to his parachute in time." He went on to say that all the crew normally wore their parachutes in flight, except for the rear gunner. The space was too cramped to wear it, so it was housed behind his seat. When calamity struck, he would have to twist himself out of his seat to reach the chute, put it on, and then struggle forward in the narrow fuselage to an exit. This tail-end Charlie didn't have enough time before she went down.

I was lost in my thoughts as I left the hanger, pondering the last moments of the bomber before she hit the water.

"Penny for them," my Dad would have said had he been there to see my reflective state. I would have told him I was thinking about how near to death he was on all his sorties, and thus how near I was to never having existed.

A short walk from the hanger stood the supersonic plane, herself. Concorde G-BBDG was the third Concorde built in Britain and one of two production test aircraft. I looked up at her symmetry, that awesome combination of grace and power. Her four Rolls Royce engines were able to propel the jet to over twice the speed of sound.

Brooklands offers a tour called the Concorde Experience: a virtual 35-minute flight in the luxury plane. I bought my boarding pass and settled into the plush grey leather seats, every one first class. The pilot for my "flight" was Captain Mike Bannister, chief Concorde pilot from 1995 to 2003. His recorded narration led his passengers through the takeoff at 246 mph. As I watched the altimeter at the front of the plane climb to over 59,000 feet, I could imagine the darkness of the sky as the plane neared the edge of the earth's atmosphere. In my mind's eye I could see the curvature of the earth as we sped at 23 miles per minute, faster than a rifle bullet, faster than the earth's rotation. The virtual engines thrust us to Mach 2, twice the speed of sound. What a triumph of engineering. Dad would have had a window seat for this sortie, of course.

A tragedy occurred in July 2000 when Concorde Air France flight 4590 burst into flames on takeoff from Charles de Gaulle airport. One hundred and twenty seconds later the aircraft crashed into a hotel in the nearly town of Gonesse, killing all one hundred and nine passengers and crew, and four people on the ground. Prior to that event, Concorde had suffered no fatalities. The crash was the beginning of the end for Concorde. There are few times in mankind's history when we take a step backwards, but such it was when the commercial era of the supersonic jet ended.

Concorde took her last flight over the Atlantic on October 24, 2003. Captain Mike Bannister was at the controls, and after he brought her safely down at London's Heathrow, he and his copilot opened the cockpit windows and waved the Union Jack.

On July 7, 2005, Old Buggerlugs was airborne over the Atlantic again. Mum and I were on the beach at Troon. I carried the maroon wide-mouthed canister holding his ashes. We had been to his favorite places—the Clubhouse of Royal Troon, from whose ornate interior we had watched Tom Weiskopf walk up the eighteenth to win the 1973 Open; and the woods at Fullarton, where the wildflowers reflected the season—a carpet of snowdrops as the winter ended, crocuses, then bluebells and daffodils in the spring, and in the summer daisies and foxgloves.

At the fourteenth green of Royal Troon, where Dad holed-in-one, there was rain in the air, a light, almost imperceptible moisture that misted the windshield. Mum and I sat in the car waiting for a twosome to finish the hole. Margery held Sid's ashes tightly on her lap, asking for a running commentary. She was by then registered blind, having lost her vision to uveitis and glaucoma.

"Now what are you doing?"

"Waiting for these two gents to putt out the hole, then I'll dash out there and scatter."

"Don't you need an umbrella?" She had heard the intermittent swoosh of the wiper blades.

"No, not wet enough for that. I won't melt." I seized my moment when the pair walked to the next tee, their windbreakers slick with rain. I poured a portion of the ashes on the grass beside the green.

"No ashes on the putting surface," the Club Secretary had cautioned.

And then we were on the beach in front of Marine View Court, the ever-present wind a force to be reckoned with. I had supported Mum's elbow as we walked down the concrete ramp to the sands. The curve of the South Beach hugged the bay. Looking west we saw the brooding shape of Ailsa Craig; toward the northwest the lighthouse of Lady Isle blinked at us; and beyond that, the Isle of Arran, the high peak of Goatfell plainly visible.

Mother held a moistened finger skyward, just as she did before lining up her drives on the golf course, to test the wind's direction. Always the pragmatist, she called to me, "Keep the wind behind you," good advice when scattering ashes.

Dad's last Atlantic patrol. His final flight. I did, and lofted the last of the ashes to catch the wind. His last sortie—Dad's last Atlantic patrol. His final flight.

Bless Your Little Cotton Socks

That Thursday in November 2005 was a usual busy day in the operating room; six patients scheduled to have surgery for their breast cancer. While I performed surgery, the OR had a hushed calm, a soft silence interrupted only by the rhythmic whoosh of the anesthesia machine. No music from the radio, I like it quiet; I like to focus. It's always been that way, even in medical school.

Four days hence on Monday would be my forty-eighth birthday; my partner Pam and I planned a trip to New York City to celebrate. My flight to meet her in Rochester, NY, was scheduled to leave St. Louis the following evening. I smiled to myself under my mask when I thought about it—our first trip since our wedding and my first birthday we would share. A highpoint of the trip was to be a carriage ride around Central Park.

Midway through the third case the phone rang, jarring the room. Bob, the circulating nurse, picked up, listened, and turned to me. "Your mother wants to talk to you," he said. I shifted a little away from the OR table and leaned towards him, taking it in. My mother Margery, in the nursing home in Troon three thousand miles away, was calling me in the middle of the day on a Thursday. Our usual day for phone calls was Sunday, not Thursday. I made a point to call before her bedtime, 8 o'clock her time, 2 o'clock my time. We checked in on one another, asked how the week was, and talked about what she was up to, what she had watched on the box, where she had walked.

Bob held the phone to my ear as I held my sterile hands to my chest. Gloved hands must not drop below waist level or they are then considered contaminated. I cocked my head to the earpiece and heard the attendant say, "Your mother wanted to talk to you today; she's feeling tired." The pause lasted a few seconds. I imagined Mum in her private room at

Westbank, sitting in her easy chair to the left of her single bed, the phone on the bedside table.

My mother came to the phone. "Hello my love." Her voice lacked its usual strength.

"Hello Mum, how are you feeling today? Jeannie said you were tired."

"I'm fine." She paused, as if contemplating her next sentence, choosing her words. "Just tired. I listened to the radio today, and some music CDs."

As she said this I imagined her fingers moving over the knobs of her CD player, the array of textures, Velcro for on/off, a button glued on for the volume control, shapes to tell her the tactile commands she could no longer see.

Most likely she had listened to her favorite singers. She had always had a penchant for soaring soprano voices ever since listening to Dame Isobel Baillie in Manchester in the thirties singing with the Halle Orchestra. The Scottish soprano Dame Isobel was renowned for her rendition of Handel's *Messiah*—she sang it over a thousand times during her career—and hearing her sing "I Know That My Redeemer Liveth," would make anyone feel that much closer to God. Her voice has been described as silvery and angelic and she was the first British singer ever to perform at the Hollywood Bowl.

"But how are *you*, my sweet? You have a birthday coming up." Behind me I had a patient on the table, so the conversation couldn't last long.

Yes, another birthday—in New York, no less. We're looking forward to our trip." My brow furrowed. "Is there anything wrong?"

"No, love. I'm just tired." I believed her.

"Well, I think at ninety-one you're allowed to be a little tired. Why don't you take a nap before your tea?"

She agreed it was a good idea. Before we signed off she said, "Call me Saturday, my pet." I promised I would, knowing that I would talk to her again on my birthday as well, our habitual birthday call in which she recited the tenuous last month of my life in utero before she delivered her preemie only child by C-section.

The room listened as I told her I loved her, Bob still holding the phone to my ear. When we'd said goodbye, Bob returned the handset to the phone on the wall and I resumed the operation. Back to my previous concentration, I didn't think about our conversation again that day.

Pam and I were married the month before. We chose Toronto because I knew the city well, having completed my fellowship in Buffalo, just over the border. Toronto is a vibrant, cosmopolitan city; it is also LGBT-friendly. Pam and I had met on the Internet—PerfectMatch.com—some six weeks before the wedding. It was a whirlwind romance, a flurry of emotions, joy, and travel between St. Louis and Rochester. We surgeons are accustomed to making decisions quickly and often. So the decision was not difficult. When Cupid strikes, it's hard to miss the arrow through the heart.

Pam made all the preparations. She had always wanted a ring from Tiffany, so we bought Tiffany rings, seven diamonds in each one. Her dear friend Susan, a minister, agreed to officiate. The venue was the City Hall in Toronto, a gleaming semi-lunar edifice of glass and steel, set against a backdrop of older sandstone buildings. The misty rain stopped, and rays of sunlight filtered through the clouds. As we took the taxi ride down Queen Street, I remarked, "If there were bagpipes, it would be perfect."

At this point, the taxi driver rolled down the window, and then we heard it—the strain of the pipes wafting through the air, playing "Scotland the Brave." Perfect—what serendipity!

Our ceremony was lovely. A Canadian judge had, by law, to officiate also, so she and Susan performed the ceremony together. We had written some vows of our own, combining them with vows from the Book of Common Prayer. They were strong vows; we promised to love, comfort, honor, keep, and be faithful.

Following the ceremony, before our afternoon tea at the Four Seasons, our photographer motioned us toward the Mounties lined up in a row on the green space outside the entrance. It was an idyllic scene—a happy couple, sunshine, Mounties, horses. So idyllic, in fact, that a busload of Japanese tourists unloaded and rushed over to snap the event for their photo albums. At this point, it was time to leave. We had become an event.

Throughout our tea—a small, intimate gathering—a compilation of our favorite songs was played, starting with the classic by Robert Burns, "My Love is Like a Red, Red Rose." We had two cakes—a sponge and a traditional Scottish wedding cake, which is a heavy, dense fruitcake layered with marzipan and hard icing. The tradition is that oblong pieces can be cut and mailed in specially designed boxes to loved ones who could not attend the ceremony. We sent a piece to Margery whom Pam had met that September. Along with it we included a CD of the songs played at our reception.

During that visit to Troon to meet my Mum, we treated her to dinner at her favorite Italian restaurant in town, Cecchini's. After our meal, I ran to retrieve the car from its parking space while Pam stood with her on the curb on Portland Street, supporting her on one arm. Mum steadied herself with her other arm on her white stick. She turned to Pam and squeezed her elbow. "It's okay for me to go now, now that Diane has found you. You are the right one."

Pam smiled at this sentiment just as I eased the car up to the curb. We helped her into the back seat, my hand on her head as usual to protect it from the doorjamb. We reversed the process when helping her out of the car on our return to Westbank. I held her elbow as she supported herself on the handrail, Mum feeling for the wall as we walked down the corridor. In her room, its walls hung with her oil paintings and watercolors, we helped her undress, pulled her nightie on over her head, and tucked her into bed. I hugged her, feeling her boney shoulders, and gave her a kiss. "Nightie, night, sweet pea," she said.

"Night, night; sleep tight," I echoed one of her phrases from my childhood. Pam and I returned to our room at the Marine Hotel, relieved that she seemed relatively stable.

On Saturday 12th November, while preparing for our flight to New York City, I called Mum from Pam's house in Rochester. The phone jangled for a minute before I replaced the receiver. I turned to Pam, "She must be in the bathroom or sitting on the lounge. I'll call in a few minutes." We continued packing for our afternoon flight. On my second call again there was no answer, but on the third I heard the voice of her attendant on the line. "Hello, is this Diane?"

"Yes, Jeannie, I'm calling to talk with my mother. She was feeing tired a few days ago." There was a moment's silence on the line, then, "I'm sorry to have to tell you, your mum passed away this morning. She had just asked me for a cup of tea, and when I brought it back to her, she was gone. It must have been very quick." After a brief pause, she continued, "We tried to reach you in St. Louis, but there was no answer."

A myriad of thoughts competed for attention in my brain. That's why she had called on Thursday. She knew we wouldn't talk on my birthday. She'd had a premonition. She really *was* tired. All I could muster was a garbled answer through a tight throat, my chin trembling. "Thanks for letting me know. We'll be there as soon as we can."

We managed to arrange flights to arrive on Monday, my birthday. As we sorted though Margery's belongings in her room at Westbank, I noted her CD player on the bedside table. Her favorite CDs were on the ledge below—Charlotte Church, Maria Callas, and Lesley Garrett. Opening the lid of the CD player, we found our compilation wedding CD she must have listened to. Beside it was the box that had contained the slice of wedding cake. It was empty. She had savored the cake. She had been there in spirit to enjoy our idyllic day.

I thought back to our conversation four days before, when we talked in the operating room. After she and I said our loving goodbyes, she ended with her usual blessing, "Bless your little cotton socks."

Epilogue

The Bench

Mum's funeral service was a lot like Dad's. Since they passed away only five months apart, I could recall what arrangements we had ordered for Sidney and replicated the list. When Mum and I shopped for Dad's casket, she insisted the only criterion was that it "burned easily." Her cremation service was held at Holmsford Bridge crematorium near Irvine, the same town where I had been born. The picture windows of the chapel looked out onto fields and the River Irvine. In the summer, when Dad passed, there had been rabbits lurching across the green swathe; for Mum, as winter approached, the grass was yellowed and frost-tipped.

Reverend Mungavin, the Rector of St. Ninian's who knew my mother well, talked about Margery's qualities, about how she was intolerant of fools and had high standards, which was a euphemism for her hard-to-please character. We sang the 23rd Psalm to Crimmond's melody, her favorite. For this funeral, of course, Pam was with me. My support. My rock.

Following the service the curtains to the left of her casket parted and she slid into the flames. I remember the first cremation I attended, my Dad's Aunt Frances. The format was the same: the curtains parted, and Great Auntie's casket moved towards the heat, but that time, perhaps because of where I was sitting, I could see the amber glow and had not been prepared for that amount of reality.

The mourners came back to Westbank to raise a glass to Margery or sip a soothing cup of tea. Everyone was solicitous and caring, speaking in gentle tones. A few murmured how sad it was they both passed in such a short span.

I countered that they died five months apart in order to continue the argument. Hearing this, one woman stared at me a moment, then flung her head back, laughing. "Oh, that's a good one, Diane." I refilled her schooner with Harvey's Bristol Cream, while she shook her head, still giggling.

When the ashes were returned to me a few days later, again in a wide-mouthed maroon plastic container, Pam and I scattered them in the places she loved: the curving beach of the South Bay and the woods at Fullarton.

With neither parent being buried, cemetery plots and headstones seemed pointless. Rather, the esplanade at Troon is flanked by strategically placed wooden benches, resting places for those walking along the prom, and remembering the hundreds of walks my parents and I took together, a bench seemed the perfect memorial.

The resting place commemorating Margery and Sidney can be found near Westbank overlooking the sweeping South Bay. In the near distance is Royal Troon Clubhouse, and in the far distance, the Heads of Ayr. A plaque mounted on the top slat bears their names and my dedication, *In loving memory of Sidney and Margery Radford from their daughter Diane.*

I imagine them sitting there, side by side, enjoying the view, listening to the sound of the birds and the waves, and watching the gulls ride the thermals.

Acknowledgements

I have many people to thank who have helped and supported me during the conception, gestation and birth of this book:

- Margery and Sidney of course, Margery for supplying the material, and Sidney for supplying the dimples I inherited.

- My teachers at Brooklands, Troon Primary, and Marr College, especially Douglas Cotter, who loved Masefield's poetry as much as my mother.

- The faculty of the Harvard Writers' Course led by Julie Silver MD, for their critiques of individual essays, their encouragement, and support. Of the faculty, special mention goes to Rusty Shelton, whose team built my website www.DianeRadfordMD.com, and designed the book cover, and to Lisa Tener, for editorial help, for her program *Bring Your Book to Life*, and for being such a great cheerleader for *Bless Your Little Cotton Socks*.

- Peter Foyle of Framework Gallery, Portland St., Troon, for befriending Margery, framing her paintings for exhibition, for granting permission to me to use his paintings as a backdrop for my website, and for allowing me to use the painting "Reflections of Troon" to introduce Part Six of this book.

- Joy Melville and Alison Hollis for providing additional details about their parents Mary and Alastair Frew, and how Margery and Mary met.

- Sheena Dodds for supplying details about Dodds of Troon.

- Bobbi Linkemer for her advice and encouragement.

Special thanks are due to Jeanne Wilson for the final edits to the book and her suggestions for improvement.

I am indebted to Donna Heckler for introducing me to Jeanne Wilson, to AuthorHouse™, and for being a more-than-capable midwife through the last trimester.

Diane Radford

Lastly, to Pamela Evans, for reading drafts when asked, laughing out loud at parts of the manuscript, and crying for others, and for her never-ending belief in my abilities.

I appreciate everyone who has touched this book in some way, either literally or figuratively.

About the Author

Diane Radford grew up in the Scottish coastal town of Troon, the only child of Margery and Sidney Radford. Troon, a town of long sweeping beaches, 13,000 people and six golf courses, shaped Diane's upbringing, as much as did her mother's eccentricities. When Diane was aged four, Margery declared she was "underfoot," and sent her off to school. An advantage of this early start in education was her entry into University of Glasgow Medical School at the age of sixteen.

Diane went on to specialize in breast cancer surgery, and has had a distinguished career in both academic surgery and private practice. She came to the United States in 1985 to pursue her surgical oncology fellowship, arriving with seven suitcases and her golf clubs. She has been listed as one of the "Best Doctors in America" every year since 1996, and is also one of America's "Top Doctors."

An accomplished speaker, she has presented to both lay and professional audiences, numbering from a hundred to many thousands. She is the author of numerous academic research papers and book chapters, has been quoted in many online media articles and print media, and has appeared on TV discussing breast cancer related topics. She is a staff breast surgical oncologist at the Cleveland Clinic in Cleveland, Ohio, and resides in Highland Heights with her spouse, their dogs Snickers and Heidi, and Buttercup the tabby.

Her essays have appeared in the *Chicken Soup for the Soul* series.

Despite all these many achievements, however, she is and always will be Margery Radford's little girl.

Endorsements

"Bless Your Little Cotton Socks is medicine for the spirit. Diane Radford's charming essays blend humor with heart in just the right doses to provoke simultaneous laughter and tears. Quirky characters and vivid descriptions whisk the reader to another time and place, where simple truths are revealed in the seemingly unremarkable events of everyday life, and where the ordinary becomes extraordinary. Don't be surprised if long dormant childhood memories come flooding back or if you find yourself smiling long after you put the book down. It's a feel-good slice of life that's just what the doctor ordered."

—Ann Pietrangelo, author of *Catch That Look* and *No More Secs!*

"Diane Radford's *Bless Your Little Cotton Socks* is a refreshing change from the usual childhood memoir. You won't find abuse and neglect and misery anywhere between its pages. You will find laugh-out-loud moments of her account of living on the beautiful west coast of Scotland with a quirky mother and a kind and patient father. A fabulous read. Funny, poignant, brilliant!"

—Melanie Milburne, USA Today best-selling romance author

"What a delight to read! Exceptionally written, beautifully told, these stories will bring smiles to your face as you travel with Dr. Diane Radford and her mum through their various houses and experiences in Scotland. A book to savor and read again and again, it will leave you anxious to call your mum for a chat."

—Donna Heckler, International Book Award finalist

CPSIA information can be obtained
at www.ICGtesting.com
Printed in the USA
LVOW10*1118180117
521379LV00001B/17/P